INTERIORS

INTERIORS

MIN HOGG
WENDY HARROP
AND
THE WORLD OF
INTERIORS

FOREWORD BY MARK HAMPTON

Clarkson N. Potter Inc./Publishers NEW YORK
DISTRIBUTED BY CROWN PUBLISHERS, INC.

Frontispiece Walls lined with ruby-red silk damask
and framed in gilded moulding are characteristic of the solid formality and
grandeur of the late-Victorian Brodsworth House in Yorkshire. The crystal bell-pull
is an elegantly confident detail – and a poignant reminder of days gone by.

Page eight Every available inch of this wall in a château in Burgundy
has been painted to create a sophisticated *trompe-l'oeil*. The limited selection of
colours – muted greys, greens and ochres – painted directly on to wooden
panelling, has a remarkable freshness after nearly three hundred years.

Text Min Hogg with Isabelle Anscombe
Art Direction Wendy Harrop with Mary Evans
Project Editor Cortina Butler
Production Michel Blake, Charles James
Editorial Assistants Elaine Collins, Jane Harcus
Assistant Designers Mark Phillips, Peter Cross

Published in the United States of America by
Clarkson N. Potter, Inc.,
distributed by Crown Publishers, Inc.,
225 Park Avenue South,
New York, New York 10003,
and represented in Canada by the
Canadian MANDA Group.

Published in Great Britain as
The World of Interiors: A Decoration Book
by Conran Octopus Limited.

CLARKSON N. POTTER, POTTER and colophon are trademarks of
Clarkson N. Potter, Inc. Publishers.

Manufactured in Italy

Library of Congress Cataloging-in-Publication Data

Hogg. Min.
    Interiors / by Min Hogg. Wendy Harrop. and The World of Interiors.
    p.256   318 × 235mm
    Selections from the magazine. The World of Interiors.
    Includes index.
    1. Interior decoration. 2. Interior architecture. I. Harrop,
Wendy. II. World of interiors. III. Title.
NK2130.H56 1988
728--dc19   88-15225
                                         CIP

    ISBN 0-517-57106-4

            10 9 8 7 6 5 4 3 2 1
            First American Edition

ACKNOWLEDGMENTS

The authors and publishers wish to thank all the
owners and designers of the rooms that are featured in this book.

Their thanks to the Paris Editor of *The World of Interiors*,
Marie-France Boyer, and to the authors of the original features in the
magazine: Jacques Almira, Colin Amery, Angela Arnim, Helen Barnes,
Priscilla Boniface, Marie-France Boyer, Charles Bricker, Richard Buckle,
Ros Byam Shaw, Mirabel Cecil, Alec Cobbe, Ronnie Cooke, Roderick Coupe,
Ilse Crawford, Michaela Dunworth, Kate Dyson, Jutta Fischer,
Desmond FitzGerald, Olda FitzGerald, Nicholas Fleming, Flora Fraser,
Stephen Gardiner, Christophe Gibbs, Jonathan Glancey, Christophe Gollut,
Desmond Guinness, Dinah Hall, Mark Hampton, Anthony Hards,
Nicholas Haslam, Clare Henry, Annabel von Hofmannsthal,
Beauregard Houston-Montgomery, Susanna Johnston, Stephen Long,
Jane Lott, George Melly, Teddy Millington Drake, Guy Nevill,
Anne O'Connor, P. J. O'Rourke, Jaime Parlade, Mariquita Perez, Stephen Pitt,
Peter Reid, Betty di Robilant, Byron Rogers, Doris Saatchi, Elisabeth Selse,
David Sexton, Brian Sewell, Bénédicte Siroux, Geraldine Smith-Parr,
Matteo Spinola, John Stefanidis, James Stevens Curl, Barbara Stoeltie,
Deyan Sudjic, Douglas Sutherland, Christopher Simon Sykes,
Georgia Tennant, Myles Thoroton Hildyard, Megan Tresidder,
Michael Trinnick, John Vaughan, John Vere Brown, Simon Verity,
David Vicary, Graham Vickers, Tim Willis and Diana Winsor.

They also thank the photographers: Bill Batten, Roland Beaufre,
Tim Beddow, Michael Boys, Richard Bryant, Dan Cornish,
Richard Davies, Jacques Dirand, Chris Drake, Peo Eriksson, Max Forsythe,
Clive Frost, David Gamble, Isidoro Genovese, Jean Pierre Godeaut,
François Halard, Dennis Krukowski, Lucinda Lambton, Tom Leighton,
Arabella McNair Wilson, James Merrell, David Montgomery,
James Mortimer, Karen Radkai, Deidi von Schaewen,
Fritz von der Schulenburg, Ingalill Snitt, Kevin Summers,
Christopher Simon Sykes, Marco de Valdivia, John Vaughan,
John Vere Brown and James Wedge.

Lovers of architecture and decoration have a kind of patron saint in *The World of Interiors* and its founders, Min Hogg and Wendy Harrop. This patron saint, extraordinary in every way, comes equipped with a flying carpet, an encyclopaedic frame of reference and a golden eye, all of which enable Miss Hogg and Miss Harrop to rid a two-dimensional surface of its traditional limitations. For this, we must be eternally grateful. In their hands, the printed page conveys light and color and detail in a narrative way that is both exciting and enchanting. These exquisite pages are also terribly informative. They present a view so still and penetrating that one never feels the frustration of not actually being there. Instead, it is possible to return again and again to that retreat on the Loire, that villa in Tuscany or that cottage in Oxfordshire. The secret personalities of houses and palaces alike are miraculously revealed. The spirit of the past fills what would otherwise be deserted spaces, and the spirit of the present becomes gentler and more appealing under their spell. Regardless of one's mood, everything appears to be perfect in their world. It is a perfection of their own invention.

Where does the ability to create this perfect view come from? First of all, I suppose, it comes from that rarest of qualities – originality. The subject matter is sometimes serious, sometimes playful. It is frequently whimsical, but it is always informative. The contrasts are dazzling. Great richness on one page gives way to stark simplicity on another. Hapsburgian grandeur shifts effortlessly to rustic charm. Continents and centuries are spanned. At times there is the heartstopping sensation of being in a time machine. The thrill of discovery leaps from every page.

The way people collect, the way they live, the innermost atmosphere of their private surroundings are touchingly depicted. There is a reverence for the homely and the well worn. The acts of creation that go into the places that people call home are celebrated and elevated with humor and respect, and beauty is found everywhere. None of this would be possible without an inspired aesthetic sense, and Min Hogg's originality and that of her partner is exceeded only by their aesthetic genius. It has a habit-forming effect. More is never enough. Less is unthinkable. Perhaps this will be the first of, say, a million books. Two million? We can only pray.   MARK HAMPTON

INTRODUCTION

This is a book in celebration of interior decoration: an exploration of the eight major decorative styles, and the circumstances that contribute to the way we regard our houses and how we live in them. To have subdivided all the glories of interior design into a mere eight categories is shockingly presumptuous, but the choices have been made, and – minor omissions apart – they are fundamental.

The pictures tell their own story, but to draw the reader right into each room, and to spotlight the elements and thought processes that have gone into its creation, every photograph or series of pictures is discussed separately in the text.

All but one of the eight chapters is introduced by an *afficionado* of the style described. Nobody can clutter a room more beautifully than antique dealer Stephen Long. His shop in Fulham Road in London is nearly as full of delicious objects as his nearby house. The decorator, architect, furniture and fabric designer John Stefanidis has interior-designed, renovated or built so many houses in the Greek Islands over the last thirty years, that he has just about perfected the art of living in a hot climate. Nicholas Haslam is the very antithesis of the decorator who is merely good with fabrics and colour. His originality as a practitioner is matched only by his encyclopaedic knowledge of the subject. Doris Saatchi has built, with her husband, one of the world's greatest collections of modern art. She practises what she preaches about living with minimalist decoration.

Henry, seventeenth Earl of Pembroke, lives at Wilton House near Salisbury, owned by his family since the sixteenth century. As the present custodian he is bound by his responsibility for preserving his ancestral home for his son and future generations.

The photographer and painter John Vere Brown has a rare gift for room-making, a blessing since he moves house with alarming frequency. Each time he unpacks his posessions he invariably achieves anew the impression that the things have been arranged that way, in that room, for decades, wearing and fading their way into the epitome of what can only be called shabby chic. Simplicity is the creed by which the designer Terence Conran lives and breathes. For him, the notion that less is best in decoration overrides all other possibilities.

The only chapter not introduced by a practitioner of the decorative style is Eccentric – but then, by definition, these home makers have nothing in common, except their individuality. The writer Elizabeth Wilhide takes an outsider's view about what sparks off some of their flights of fancy.

Elaborate or basic, ornate or stripped bare, Nordic or Mediterranean, there is one thread linking all the rooms photographed in this book – each one is an example of excellence within its type.

As co-editors and designers of *The World of Interiors* magazine since its launch, Wendy Harrop and I are often asked if we think the current craze for interior decoration is a passing phase. We believe that in whatever direction fashion may drift in the future, beautiful decoration will always be one of life's greatest pleasures.   MIN HOGG

CLUTTERED

A single object may be taken as a starting point for the
entire decoration of a room, but for a compulsive collector it is
the whole jumble – furniture, art, china, treasures, personal
mementoes – that is the essence of the design.
There is rarely a contrived scheme or method to such interior
design, it is more often a combination of beautiful and
idiosyncratic items – just as carefully selected as a single
object in a minimal interior – which come together to create
a highly personal and enchanting scenario which would
be a nightmare to move.

Vistas and reflections dominate the house that Sir John Soane,
architect, antiquarian and insatiable collector, built as museum and home in the early
nineteenth century. Plaster portrait medallions, paintings, antique fragments
and books, presented on different coloured backgrounds and carefully lit, frame the
doorways between dressing room, study and dining room.

I do not much like this word clutter. It has a pejorative tone. I read recently the phrase 'elegant clutter' used to describe Diana Vreeland's apartment in New York. But the Oxford English Dictionary gives the word no cosy connotations, not even a suspicion of charm or elegance. Clutter, it says sternly, is 'a disorderly assemblage of things' ... 'crowded confusion' ... 'a clotted mass'. I discovered also the excellent seventeenth-century word cluttery, meaning 'disorder and dirt'.

As a style of decorating, however, clutter has an honourable history going back at least to the reign of Good King William and dear Queen Adelaide, and certainly cluttered rooms existed long before 1830. We can imagine them occupied by convivial rectors grown rich on pluralism, by amateur inventors with their combined libraries and laboratories, and by spinsters and dowagers surrounded by the souvenirs of a lifetime.

What was perhaps new in the second quarter of the nineteenth century was that the public or entertaining rooms of both modest and grand houses began to fill up with furniture and bric-à-brac. All this embryo clutter converged in the middle of rooms. Nevertheless I suspect that the present orthodox opinion that in the eighteenth century *all* the furniture in *every* room was *always* pushed against the wall is a lot of fashionable claptrap.

By the end of Queen Victoria's reign, as we all know, if somebody wanted to glide about in what had once been called rooms of parade, it meant going on a species of assault course round whole clumps of potted palms, sociables, and occasional tables awash with framed photographs.

Only a decade later at the beginning of George V's reign there were already signs of change and Queen Mary set vigorously to work to simplify the Royal palaces. However, I know of one instance when, on expert advice, the Queen cleared out all the junk in a room in Buckingham Palace without telling the King, who, when he found out, made her put it all back!

In fashionable circles in those two hectic decades between the World Wars – indeed in all circles of people who wished to appear Up-to-date and Thoroughly Modern – the stripped-to-the-bone look was all the rage. Down came the Nottingham lace and up went the hessian. Almost all pictures were banished. A mass of knick-knacks would have looked very odd on a streamlined side-table veneered in Empire woods or on one of Mrs Maugham's dubious pickled commodes. For the rich the only touches of lushness were the bosomy flower arrangements of Mrs Spry. Here is a description of a room (as late as 1939) by the great historian of taste James Laver. An imaginary cultivated couple of modest means have '... plain distempered walls, straight-lined open bookcases, chairs comfortable, but without any unnecessary upholstery, covered with plain, coarse canvas. Their carpet is self-coloured harmonizing with the tone of the room. Their lampshades are made of plain sheets of parchment. On their walls they have one picture: a varnished Underground poster. Good Taste.' Those who remember those sparse rooms can understand why reaction set in.

There were exceptions already among the *avant-garde*. Pioneer connoisseurs of the Regency had already packed in the sphinxes and obelisks, the marble busts and the ormolu. Already also, a trickle of 'amusing' domes of wax fruit, Berlin woolwork of overblown roses and papier mâché painted with sad-eyed dogs was infiltrating many a smart interior as war loomed.

The notion of clutter – and its boon-companion, Wit – as a decorative theme was spotted and plugged by the English edition of *House and Garden* (bi-monthly in those rationed days) well before the Festival of Britain in 1951. Not for nothing were a revived pair of white and gold Staffordshire figures of a lion and a unicorn one of the official souvenirs of that extraordinary show. In 1959, Osbert Lancaster brought up to date his brilliant pre-war collection of satirical essays on interior design, *Home Sweet Homes*. He called his wicked version of clutter 'Neo Victorianism' because clutter then was mostly of Victorian artefacts and aimed to revive the cosiness of that era. It was not the mad mixture of all periods popular today. Lancaster blamed the style on the cheap second-hand furniture couples were forced to buy because most new stuff was For Export Only. 'So strong', he writes, 'was the character of these pieces that, like a faint touch of garlic, they completely transformed any interior into which they were introduced. One Victorian work-table ... heralded the arrival of a whole summer of ottomans, Aubussons, beadwork fire-screens, Martin engravings, lustres, portières and Bohemian glass ...'

Nevertheless, the style of clutter-mania as we know it took a long time to catch on. John Fowler, on whom the look has often been unfairly blamed, was sparing with his pictures and objects, and his own rooms were positively sparse by today's standards. He was also very economical with the chintz with which his followers smother their rooms.

True clutter is very different from those artfully arranged tablescapes, piles of expensive books and endless buttons and bows aimed to give an instant lived-in look. It is based on the often unconscious acquisitiveness of many of the Human Race who cannot resist making jackdaw nests for themselves with things which have taken their random fancy. Another sort of clutter springs from the passion of the dedicated collector who will always find space for yet another incunabulum, stuffed bird or snuff box.

We may note all these themes in this chapter of the book. When I was squinting through my magnifying glass at the O.E.D's harsh definitions, I flattered myself that they did not remotely apply to *me*. Then I found a couple of my rooms had been cruelly selected as illustrations. These photographs were taken eight years ago. To my horror, looking at these same corners today, I found the breathing space (not generous, I admit, even then) has become even more clogged. Brackets now climb the walls to support even more junk, yet more surfaces have become packed with books and objects. I now realise I am a terminal case of cluttery even though the disease has lasted many years – and I may last a few more.

Although I suspect that the style's days of high fashion are already over, this section of the book is a Grim Warning to those who may still want to inject cluttery artificially and all at once. They will probably catch the disease in real earnest and though the symptoms can be fun, the infection is almost certainly fatal.

A ROOM WHERE IT IS ALWAYS AFTER DARK

In a flat consisting of two large rooms, the owner, who likes plenty of space for entertaining, has made both of them into bed-sitters. One is bright and summery, the

other, *above*, is a warm night-time room where the shutters are permanently closed. Finely detailed Piranesi prints and an oil painting are set off by plain red-laquered walls which glow in the artificial light. Cushions made from antique textiles and needlework camouflage the bed.

CONJURING SPACE FROM A STUDIO APARTMENT

Richard Lowell-Neas, New York decorator and *trompe-l'oeil* artist, lives in a single room only 22 foot square. To increase its size visually, two huge mirrors face each other,

one framed by painted draperies to suggest a room beyond. The fold-down bed is concealed behind one of the pair of recycled cupboard doors, saved from a Paris hotel demolition, that flank the mirror. Large items of furniture and a profusion of patterns create a deceptive grandeur.

COLOUR AND PATTERN LIGHTEN A PANELLED ROOM

Frankly tattered, antique silk curtains divide this French drawing room. They have been given a new lease of life with a backing of modern 'tree of life' patterned chintz, used

also on the buttoned sofa. Any room lined from floor to ceiling in dark, carved panelling such as this, could be a little sombre, but splashes of brilliant colour enliven the scene – yellow silk cushions, crimson velvet sofa, Persian carpets and an occasional gleam of ornamental gilding.

A MAKESHIFT TOWER FOR EXTRA CLUTTER

In order to inject even more surfaces into his small London sitting room to hold his possessions, the owner built bookcases jutting into the room like a tower. This practical arrangement replaced an unattractive partition, preserving the cornice. The reverse of the construction forms a little entrance hall. To crowd vivid green-painted shelves against walls clad in taupe-coloured stamped velvet and crowned with a cornice in Rameses red, is a daring and original use of colour having much in common with grand interiors of the past rather than following the present-day penchant for decorating in a single pastel shade.

PRECIOUS OBJECTS IN A FRIENDLY SETTING

The intensity of the emerald green chosen by Allen Murphy for the panelling of his drawing room in Long Island, has a unifying effect upon the varied collections of precious objects arranged against it. He has used a single dramatic sweep of dragged colour – rather than accentuating the mouldings with a different shade – with black marble cornice, skirting (base) boards and door-frames for dramatic contrast. This is the display of an avid collector, dedicated to the exquisite and the rare; junk shop finds are not at all his idiom. But far from looking like a chilly museum, this room has been made to appear friendly and inviting.

DELIBERATE METHOD IN THE APPARENT DISORDER

Dawn shopping raids on street markets, and an unerring eye for the intriguing and the beautiful, go some way to explain the sheer mass of objects in antique-dealer Stephen Long's London house. But there is far more to his decorative method than collecting pretty things. He believes in starting with a bold statement: here, the Chinese-yellow walls, reddish tortoiseshell cornice, and the bookcase painted to match. Having laid down some strong lines, he then softens them with the clutter – the process is like building up a picture with layers of paint. This owner has the extra advantage of being able to rid himself of things he has cooled towards, by selling them in his shop.

Close inspection reveals that many of these predominantly pre-1820 objects come in pairs. On the sofa-table nearly everything has a twin and their scale is nicely contrasted by the two huge blue ironstone jars which stand behind. On the *faux* tortoiseshell chimney-piece, *overleaf*, symmetry is even more pronounced in his arrangement of rare pottery and china, portrait busts, jugs and a pair of hand-held face screens, painted to resemble open books. The shades on the creamware candlesticks are changed as the day draws on – green looks good by daylight but red is better when the candles are alight.

1

2

3

4

5

6

COLLECTIONS DISPLAYED

Ways of display are as many and various as the objects that are collected. In a Venetian palazzo a nest of chairs is casually balanced on and around a table (1). Antique miniatures (8) crowd the panelled wall of a Long Island games room. A museum owner's hand-painted fans (12), strewn across a bed, suggest that his house has reached saturation point.

For one confessed accumulator, ornamental bird cages satisfy a need to show function bowing to form (9). An antiques dealer sees her bold assortment of instruments (5) as a living composition in historical form.

7

8

9

10

11

12

There need not be anything very unusual about an arrangement: glasses filled with violets set dramatically against a vivid painted backcloth (2); a simple grouping of porcelain, ivory, marble, and neoclassical busts (3);

china on a painted dresser (10); a perfect array of ivory-handled magnifying glasses and letter openers (4).

The mantelpiece is often central – from the rococo elegance of an overmantel and its stark display of seven-

teenth- and nineteenth-century temples (6), or the cool white marble Louis XVI fireplace which supports a fine collection of china (11), to the more rustic, stone mantel (7) holding handcrafted terracotta figures.

ANTIQUE COLOURS
IN A CHELSEA BEDROOM

The green of the china on this London mantelpiece is a particular shade much favoured in the eighteenth century. Old pottery and porcelain are among the few items handed down by previous generations that have not faded, and provide excellent guides to decorating colours of the past. The owner used this green to paint a Louis

XVI trellis design on to the hessian wall-covering in his bedroom. The effect approximates *imprimé sur chaîne*, a technique in which pattern is printed on to the warp before the fabric is woven.

The display well illustrates the owner's maxim that if you cannot afford the very best, then crowd it up. Bookcases deliberately crammed full are as important to the scheme as the thoughtfully hung pictures beside a glass-cased pheasant.

A DECORATIVE PASSION
FOR FISHING AND FISH

The owner of this London flat is a keen angler, and her items of fishing tackle, including antique rods and nets, are displayed as ornaments. Reels fill one shelf of the dresser, stuffed and carved fish swim above the fireplace, and frames of fishing flies lean against the walls.

All the elements in the dining room are

piscatorial: the books are about angling, the Doulton plates on the dresser show fishermen, and the pictures on the wall are of fish and anglers, including, above the black marble mantelpiece, Millais' portrait of his daughter after she had successfully landed eleven Scots salmon. The pieces of oak Arts and Crafts furniture in the room are perfectly in character with such a rural theme, extolling as they do the virtues of rustic honesty and skill in handling nature.

EARTHENWARE PLATES PERFECTLY DISPLAYED

Overleaf Be it tapestry, T'ang or tortoiseshell, all inveterate collectors with a particular speciality face the same problem: how best to display the objects they have found so irresistible. In the dining room of a Provençal manor house an admirable solution has been found for a rich collection of glazed pottery. These include deep green Lunéville plates, asparagus Barbotines and brown antique vermicelli-patterned Faucon plates from the pottery at Aptes. The owner has used his expertise as a former cabinet-maker to design and execute a 30 foot bank of narrow shelving, with pronounced uprights, on which to arrange the rows of plates amassed by his wife. The method of presentation heightens the decorative impact of the collection and the plates are kept out of harm's way.

HOMOGENEOUS MIXTURE OF FULL CREAM

If you are a magpie at heart, the mantelpiece is a wonderful place to display your prettiest pieces. Here are four arrangements using not just the mantelshelf but also the wall above, to show off the rich delicacy of English creamware.

Developed by Josiah Wedgwood around 1765 and soon copied by many other potteries, creamware was used for everything from tea pots to jelly moulds. It is often decorated with pinks and purples, but some of the loveliest pieces are uncoloured, with feather or shell edges and fine moulding for interest. Its pale beauty can be displayed against a lively coloured background, but it is equally beautiful against a plain colour. Any type of china can be mixed if the colours, shapes and textures are complementary.

THE VICTORIAN HEYDAY OF THE WHATNOT

The whatnot, first introduced in the Regency period, was a piece of furniture perfectly suited to the Victorians' love of clutter. Had it not existed, it would have been essential to invent it to hold and display books, ornaments, framed photographs and general knick-knacks. This one, made around 1880, is of fruitwood, with a single bottom drawer. On it are arranged pieces of Wedgwood greenware and creamware, green majolica, Rockingham plates, green glass ornaments, jugs, a tea-caddy, cake stands and a cast-iron 'bank' money-box. Like the collections on the mantelpieces, it is colour and repetition of shape that hold the objects together in harmony against a background of a mid-Victorian needlework carpet.

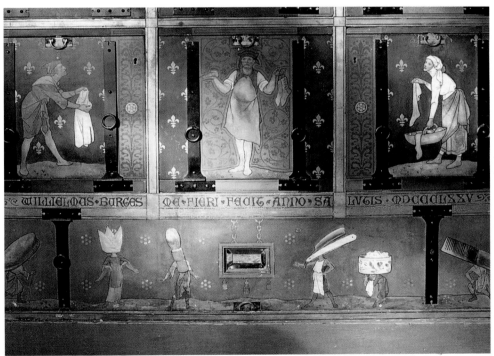

THE BEDROOM FANTASIES OF WILLIAM BURGES

Clutter came naturally to the high-Victorian Gothic fantasies of architect William Burges. Every conceivable surface of his house in Kensington, for which this furniture was originally made, was covered with painted panels, Gothic designs, stars, sunbursts and other insignia. The furniture was also carved, gilded and painted, and objects such as silver goblets or flasks were en-crusted with Roman coins, rare stones and other items he had collected. The associations are both romantic and witty. The bed is painted with scenes from 'Sleeping Beauty'; on the cabinet doors are miniature panels of flowers, complete with shadowy fairies. The wardrobe depicts the clothing of Adam after his expulsion from the Garden of Eden, but, lest one take those allusions too seriously, the panels below show Burges' hairbrush, comb, razor, and shaving brush and cream come to life.

SILHOUETTES CLIMBING THE WINDING STAIRS

A staircase is an ideal place to hang masses of pictures and other objects, especially small ones that are best viewed at close quarters. These curvaceous stairs climb five storeys of a Sussex house. The owner, who collects just about everything it is possible to collect, has chosen to hang his walls with part of his large accumulation of eighteenth- and nineteenth-century silhouettes. With so many at his disposal, he has divided and located them by subject-matter – the portrait heads are clustered on the drawing room walls and the figures are here in the stairwell. Hung close together, without concern for order or symmetry, they make an effective display.

Although silhouetted figures predominate, there is sufficient variation to rest the eye from the monochrome: to the left, a neat row of painted miniatures and, higher up, three unrelated pictures, including an elegant racehorse and jockey. The ever-expanding display has already spread down to knee level and will soon, no doubt, fill the few spaces that remain.

AN ELEGANT ARRANGEMENT ON TOMATO-RED WALLS

An ordered collection of hand-coloured, eighteenth-century topographical engravings was gathered on the owner's travels. With similar subjects, frames and mounts, this disciplined display looks satisfyingly generous without overwhelming. The pictures are hung in neat columns, with slightly less regard for horizontal regularity, against a tomato-red background. The walls were covered with five coats of glaze to achieve the desired shade.

CANARY-YELLOW CUPS
AT KING'S COLLEGE

Dadie Rylands moved into his rooms in King's College, Cambridge as a young don in 1927. Over the years they have been the setting for numberless theatrical rehearsals and literary gatherings. They are also over-flowing with the fruits of half a century of accumulation. A corner cupboard, *below right*, holds a collection of rare canary-yellow pottery, eighteenth-century glasses, an assortment of jugs and mugs, a bust of Milton, and a pair of Staffordshire zebras.

A SHRINE TO A FRENCH
SYMBOLIST PAINTER

The house in Paris where the Symbolist painter Gustave Moreau lived with his mother from 1830, has remained un-changed since his death in 1896. Shortly

before he died, he had it altered and extended to exhibit his thousands of unsold paintings and drawings. He left the house and his works to the State on condition that they be kept together.

The only part of the house that was not altered was Madame Moreau's suite of rooms. When she died in the 1880s, her son moved into them. Today they are locked away from the public and the atmosphere of a shrine prevails. A portrait of Moreau's mother hangs above the desk in his bedroom, *main picture*. His French Academy uniform lies on his bed, *top left*, covered with branches of box signifying evergreen remembrance. The walls around his bed are crammed with works by various friends. The boudoir, *below left*, contains a typically mid-nineteenth-century accretion of furnishings and memorabilia collected by Moreau to give his ideas visual impetus.

DECORATING A ROOM WITH NO VIEW

English decorator, Keith Irvine, who lives and works in New York, came home from holiday to find his view of Manhattan had been obliterated by a new building put up next door. In self-defence he glazed this big, cheerful sitting room with eight layers of strawberry red, and made it into a night-time room. The windows that now face directly on to a brick wall are masked by black mesh blinds and red linen curtains, elaborately pleated, smocked and swagged. The low ceiling is made to seem higher with an expanse of plain white paint and is bordered by a Greek-key-patterned cornice.

The room looks as though someone is in the throes of moving house, but that is just the way the family likes to live. It is not only the books stacked on the floor – there are no shelves visible for them – or the masses of cushions and myriad objects displayed on tables and whatnots. It is also the array of patterns that makes this large room so comfortably full of life: an Aubusson rug on the floor; a chair covered in antique *toile de Jouy* and another in a flowery chintz; cushions in every pattern from leopard skin to a royal crown. Even the mirror has a painting hung over of it – it all adds to the clutter. Yet there are oases of calm: the sofa upholstered in white to match the ceiling and another chair cleverly camouflaged in black lining-fabric go some way to tone down the madness.

CLASSICAL PAIRS COMPETE IN WEST LONDON

Overflowing with beautiful things, this London drawing room is also highly disciplined. It contains nothing that is not fine or specially chosen: objects that would be centre-pieces in most rooms – an antique painting, impressive classical sculpture on the hearth or French eighteenth-century furniture – compete for attention.

The architectural elements of the room are obviously cherished, particularly the deep dentil cornicing and the elegant marble fireplace. Nothing could be plainer than the choice of paintwork or the absolutely unadorned lampshades and curtains – there are none of the conventional decorator's frills here. But the consciously ornate also has its place, in the chandelier and the gilt candle sconces which echo the details of the fireplace. The decorative scheme is so tailored to the occupant's own taste that even an otherwise quite *outré* object such as the sculpture by Anish Kapoor on the left, known as 'The Brain', seems perfectly natural next to an equally large blue and white vase. The preponderance of blue, in the Oriental porcelain and in the rug, seems to pull the room together.

A sense of order is achieved by the repeated use of matching pairs of objects – the table lamps, the sconces or the vases on the mantelpiece – even the reflections of pictures in the mirrored wall by the window repeat this doubling-up effect.

HOT CLIMATE

Life can be conducted very differently when the weather
is warm and clear skies a regular occurrence. It is outward rather
than inward looking, there is rarely a need to protect against
cold winds and driving rain. As winter clothes look drab
or frowsty when the spring sun shines on them, so the interior
design styles of the temperate and northern climes look alien in
the clear light of the Mediterranean, Caribbean or tropics.
Walls are whitewashed, colours are clean and brilliant, furniture
and patterns are simple and traditional to the locality. The most
successful houses reflect their surroundings.

A pair of wide window-doors opens on to a shimmering landscape
and a terrace, shaded by olive trees and a wisteria-covered pergola, which almost
doubles the living space of this house in Tuscany. Dappled sunlight falls on to a stone
table and metal-frame reclining chairs.

n August 15, twenty seven years ago, I was one of only three foreigners on the Greek island of Patmos. There were no visitors from Athens, no tourists and no restaurants. Cruise ships and the quays for them to tie up at were unknown. The ferry from Piraeus anchored far out and its passengers were carried ashore in small boats; after the fourteen-hour journey there was a real sense of arrival.

Today, not only on Patmos but wherever there are beautiful islands, life has changed immeasurably. The intervening years have witnessed an explosion of development, with invasions of foreigners seeking the sun and something else less easily defined – perhaps the simplicity of a way of life that has largely vanished from the modern world.

Northerners were migrating south long before Goethe crossed the Alps, but when travel became cheap and speedy, holidays in hot countries became available to everyone. In the nineteenth century, people went to Italy for the 'light'; later the South of France attracted painters such as Matisse and Dufy. By the 1920s, the Riviera had been colonized by intellectuals like the Murphys, F. Scott Fitzgerald and their circle; soon after came the likes of Chanel, Colette, Cocteau and Picasso. Innumerable pleasure-seekers followed. A suntan, until then evidence of rural labour, became both the symbol of a life of leisure and a sign of good health, an association which derives particularly from the German sunworshipping and fitness cult of the 1920s.

A style for hot-climate life has evolved which is in many ways a conceit, but nevertheless a conceit worth pursuing. It is equal parts romanticism, sensuality and practicality.

In the romantic sense, hot-climate style is a way of appreciating the simple life. It is reassuring because it demonstrates that, at least in some places, things do not change that quickly. Peasant cottages and farmhouses are converted to holiday homes; some new houses copy the local vernacular. In keeping with the character of these buildings – architecture without architects – furnishings are countrified, handmade and not too grand. Whitewashed walls, tiled floors, scrubbed boards, nineteenth-century provincial furniture, pottery and local embroidery are all part of a deliberate strategy to maintain the fantasy. But such interiors are not only found in hot countries. Only a few years ago I visited a Gloucestershire farmhouse which had been left untouched for decades and was startled to find how closely it resembled some of the Patmos houses I knew so well.

In practical terms, hot-climate style is a triumph of common sense. Whitewashed walls reflect light and heat; thick walls mean cool interiors and protection from strong, hot winds (*meltemi* in Greece, *mistral* in France, *sirocco* in Italy). For houses which are generally occupied only in the warmer months, cotton furnishings are cooler than velvet and wool, and easier to wash after a prolonged absence. Shutters at the windows exclude glare and filter breezes better than curtains, which can become dusty and tattered in the wind. Draping beds with muslin cuts out bright morning light; latticed doors allow air to circulate.

But these interiors are pleasing on a more elemental level. Living in a hot country, especially for those who are not native to it, reawakens the senses. There is a tactile difference in the way 'hot' and 'cold' interiors are experienced, and hence furnished. Going about barefoot means that you can enjoy the smoothness and coolness of marble or tiles, the roughness of stone and the texture of kilims and woven cotton rugs. Hard benches with cushions mean you can sit Oriental-style with your feet up – deep-cushioned sofas would be stifling. There are those restful colours, the traditional blue, pale pink, melon, light grey and lime green which can be found on the shores of all the seas of the world.

The greatest pleasure is being out of doors. In these climates, inside and outside are drawn together. Rooms open on to terraces, once used for cultivation but now as pleasure gardens. The heat intensifies the musky scent of the tropics or the potent, lingering smell of plants such as rosemary, lavender, plumbago and jasmine which grow well in dry conditions. Simple food tastes delicious eaten outside in the shade of a vine or *canisse*; you can indulge in the sort of activities, such as having a conversation under the stars, which would be faintly ridiculous anywhere else. Above all there is the light, an almost tangible element in these climates. When I am away from Greece I miss the light.

Hot-climate style is not only an idealization of a way of life that is disappearing, but also something of a fiction. Before foreigners came to Greece, there was no bathing in the sea. The old folk on Patmos may have sun-tanned forearms and necks but even in high summer are well wrapped up in woollen vests, cummerbunds and hats. The young people much prefer modern cement-built flats to traditional island houses.

In one sense, as soon as you invade a community where you do not belong, it begins to be spoiled; locals who have travelled and lived abroad also bring back modern ideas that are unsuited to the architecture that is their heritage. There is the real fear that those of us who are intruders might ruin it for ourselves, but this anxiety has also inspired a great deal of careful and sympathetic restoration. Change is inevitable and also a benefit, as long as it is not too rapid, and as long as we are ready to learn the lessons the past has to offer.

SUNSHINE AND SHADE IN OUTDOOR ROOMS

In countries where the noon sun bleaches the colour from the landscape, outdoor rooms not only take advantage of cooling breezes, but also make the changing light part of the life of the house. In an abundant garden in southern Spain, *previous page*, a ruined Moorish watchtower stands guard over a wide terracotta-tiled terrace. Four sturdy white posts support cross-beams of pine, trained with a shady grapevine. The loggia of an Andalusian retreat, *top left*, a blend of classical and Moorish influences, blurs the edges between interior and exterior. It provides protection against the sun for both the drawing room behind and those sitting in its shade high above a valley of olive and almond trees. Cool-coloured ticking covers the wicker chairs.

The terrace of a new house overlooking the harbour entrance on the Greek island of Patmos, built to a design by John Stefanidis, has typically Greek thick stone walls and pristine whitewash. The floor is paved with a mixture of flagstones and pebbles from local beaches. The creeper, designed to cover the pergola, has not yet completed its task: in the interim, a temporary screen of split bamboo cane gives shade.

The Villa Parisi, *above*, sits feudally at the summit of a hill among the Sabine Hills north-east of Rome. Limpet-like, the church and village houses cling to its lower walls, and some of the castle's rooms look directly on to the village square. This roofed-over terrace, bathed in the afternoon light, with its profusion of plants in terra-cotta pots, curly-cane furniture, old basket chairs and matting, is used as an outdoor reception room all through the summer.

1

2

3

4

5

TAKING THE INSIDE OUT

Warm weather and clear skies that can be relied upon for at least part of the year make outdoor living, eating and even sleeping spaces a realistic proposi-

tion. In most cases, though, some protection against the elements is needed. Pergolas covered with roses (7) or split cane (1 *and* 10) protect against the sun. Twelve-foot-thick buttress walls keep a Greek island house (2)

cool inside and shade cushions propped up outside. An Indian verandah (3) is shielded from the sun by green cane blinds. Dining areas need protection against sea breezes whether in the Caribbean (6), or on Patmos (8).

6

7

8

9

10

Permanent, weatherproof seating and tables are sometimes built when the terrace is constructed (1 *and* 8), then softened with mattresses, cushions and bolsters. Alternatively, the terrace can be furnished with chairs light enough to be moved indoors in the winter months – metal-frame *chaises longues* or sofa in a Tuscan house (10), white-painted planters' chairs in India (3), or simple white and vivid blue mattress cushions on a terrace in a Greek garden (4).

A compromise between inside and outside has been reached in a glassed-over central courtyard (5). An internal open space filled with plants is especially valuable in a house in the Canary Islands which has no garden (9).

A PAIR OF SPANISH HALLS, GRAND AND DOMESTIC

Gigantic and slightly crumbling honey-coloured stone blocks give monumental scale to the entrance hall of a house on Gran Canaria, *above*. But they are all illusion, painted *à la trompe-l'oeil* on to flat walls by the French artist André Dubreuil for the owner, designer and antique dealer Christophe Gollut. The deceptively small chair, locally made stone jar and discarded shoes only serve to emphasize the seigneurial feel. The glass-panelled, dark, olive-green doors have striped cotton curtains gathered on to poles, top and bottom, to keep them from blowing around in the breeze.

In a house built on a hillside in southern Spain, *right*, the hall lies at its very core – a room of frequent passage. To one side is the drawing room, and, to the other, a courtyard and stairs down to the bedrooms. The green-painted and dog-scratched door leads on to an upper terrace. The brick tiles, laid in traditional block and herringbone patterns, come from a seventeenth-century convent burned down during the Civil War. At night, the pierced metal Moroccan lantern casts a delicate pattern on the walls.

CONTROLLING THE ELEMENTS WITH SHUTTERS AND BLINDS

Overleaf The window shutters in this Andalusian drawing room permit many degrees of openness, depending on the heat or cold. The blinds are of old blue-green striped velvet with a black and red cotton border, strung up by cords: when raised, they form a single wide swag which looks like a very deep pelmet. The fireplace, as is often the case in Andalusian houses, has been moulded out of plaster.

SHADES MADE BY SIXTY YEARS OF SUNSHINE

Pink is a favourite decorating colour in the Canary Islands, frequently seen next to outer doors and shutters painted a dark, yet brilliant green which fades over the years to the shade seen in this drawing room window, *above*. The owner scrubbed the chair rail and door surrounds clean, back to their original shade of powdery grey-blue, and covered a set of French chairs to match.

ROOMS FULL OF CLEAR ISLAND LIGHT AND COLOUR

The blue sky and clear light of Greece has crept indoors on to the woodwork and furniture of two rooms on the island of Patmos. Both have windows and shutters opening inwards and locally made sofas. An antique screen, *top*, is decorated with engravings of Ottoman costumes. The library, *right*, of a nineteenth-century merchant's house, overlooks a panorama of inlets.

AIRY RETREATS FROM STIFLING TEMPERATURES

Coolness prevails in the entrance hall of an Athenian apartment built in 1964 in the Greek Revival style for an American traveller, bibliophile and collector of antiquities. His passion for all things Hellenistic was obviously shared by his American architect, Charles Shoup, who designed the classically coffered ceiling and an abundance of refined plasterwork architectural mouldings. Throughout the building, the walls are painted white and all the floors inlaid with various geometric designs in russet, grey and white marbles. Beneath and on top of the brass-trimmed Empire table are ancient jars and urns; in the centre, an Italian Renaissance font with a domed top.

North up the dusty highway from Calcutta lies Plassey House beside a lake that was once part of the River Ganges. The brick and stucco house was built for a Western-educated Bengali nobleman with European tastes in what is best described as Indo-Palladian style. The whitewashed drawing room, *above*, is furnished with a suite of Victorian furniture covered in Belgian tapestry fabric; it was made in India in 1891 to celebrate a wedding. Refreshing draughts enter through glass-panelled doors, which give on to wide verandahs – exterior rooms that also keep out the harsh

sun. Lazily turning ceiling fans encourage the slightest breeze, and the kerosene chandelier is still used. The tiger whose head is mounted on the wall was shot by an uncle who, in old age, was eaten by another one.

TRADITIONAL ISLAND SOFAS WITH MATTRESS CUSHIONS

Overleaf Painter Teddy Millington Drake has lived on the Greek island of Patmos for twenty-five years, and his house, built in 1688 by a Russian merchant, which he restored from near dereliction with John Stefanidis, can be said to have set the standard for sympathetic Mediterranean architecture and decoration.

The soft terracotta tiled floors of this upstairs sitting room are typical of the local houses although they are now often replaced with easy-care terrazzo. The frames of the wooden sofa and *chaises longues* are copied from a traditional island design; their mattress-style cushions were made by the village midwife. The original shutters are unpainted, but treated annually with linseed oil to weatherproof them. Simple box tables of trellis set into a plain framework, made in the village to Stefanidis' design, are painted with two tones of brown that complement the plain simplicity of the tiled floor and freshly whitewashed walls.

MINT-GREEN BEAMS IN A SPANISH HOUSE

Whether to paint beamed ceilings or not is a debate that rages between purists who do not and the less strict who would. This Spanish kitchen would traditionally have had plain wooden timbers but the owner elected to paint them a mint green which has a reflectively cooling effect. The high hearth of the canopied fireplace has a tiled surface on which logs are laid without a grate. Simple local chairs with rush seats are painted yellow. The floor tiles, typical of southern Spain, were made in Malaga. Suppers are taken outside beneath a pergola.

A FLEXIBLE APPROACH TO SEATING GUESTS

When the number of diners varies, the most adaptable seating arrangement is to have two tables, as in this late nineteenth-century house on Patmos, instead of one massive piece of furniture. The simplest of ingredients have been used: hand-woven Greek cotton undercloths on the tables, black-painted party chairs of mixed design, primitive portraits, and a Victorian Greek sideboard. The floorboards are scrubbed but not waxed. The only elements of countrified sophistication are the Italian tin chandelier and the gilded looking-glass.

LATTICED WOODWORK
SUITED TO THE HUMIDITY

In hot, humid climates, latticed woodwork is both romantic and practical: while looking light and cool, perforated doors also allow free circulation of air, so discouraging damp and mould. The lattice door and walls in a windowless Greek bathroom, *left*, let in light as well as air. Bookshelves, *top*, are concealed behind a two-gauge criss-cross in a Tuscan drawing room. On a Spanish landing, *above left*, clothes are stored in airy cupboards. In a bathroom on Patmos, trellis cupboards, *above right*, have tiled tops.

THE BLUE OF THE GREEK SKY
IN A BEDROOM

Overleaf Swathes of white muslin, looped up by tapes attached at intervals to the fine metal crossbars, festoon a blue-painted four-poster bed in Greece. Another gauzy layer stretches across the top and down the back. The blue chairs are a modern copy of an original at Palladio's Villa Malcontenta near Venice. Cloth, woven in Athens, covers basic oblong tables. Strong bright light streams in from a high window; light from the door that leads on to a small courtyard, where the duck belongs, is more muted.

DESIGNER DECORATED

Sometimes there is an opportunity to decorate a house as a consistent whole, rather than leave it to evolve organically over a period of time. In a designed interior the role of each element has been carefully calculated in relation to its fellows, whether it is a wallcovering, a carpet, a piece of furniture, a pelmet or a small vase. There is a tendency towards the ornate, the finely crafted and the luxurious. The most successful top-to-toe decorated interiors reflect both the owner's personality and style *and* that of the designer – perhaps best of all when they are one and the same person. The approach is not exclusively the province of the professionals, but it requires taste, confidence, perfectionism and a professional attitude.

New York decorator Mark Hampton is a self-confessed
Anglophile who describes many of the objects in his Manhattan apartment
as holiday souvenirs from London. On a gilded table in the drawing room is a collection
of treasures with nothing to declare except their beauty, set against a unifying
background of curtains and walls in 'Old Rose' chintz from that most traditionally
English of decorating firms, Colefax and Fowler.

The last twenty years or so have witnessed a revival in taste for opulence and comfort of almost Edwardian proportions – a counter to the spareness, one might even say barrenness, of decoration, hand-in-glove with the nihilistic architecture of the modern movement that was a feature of the post-war period. This renaissance is felicitously unstructured, ordaining no specific style, and offering a multitude of ways for interior designers to display their gifts; and it is uniquely retrospective. Until these latter decades of the present century, almost anyone who built a house wanted it furnished in the latest, most up-to-the-minute style; now the past is constantly plundered for its treasures. While it must be stressed that there is no mainstream fashion in decoration – though there are fashionable clichés which have to be avoided – there are several strong influences that have directed the path of late twentieth-century decoration.

No individual, king or court, any longer sets the style of decor that will be copied the world over, as in, say, the periods of Louis XV and XVI, Napoleon, Queen Anne or George IV. Madame de Pompadour, with her superbly beautiful taste and her position as Louis XV's mistress, has probably had the most pervading influence. She transformed the overawing splendour of the style of the previous reign with the flowing lines in rooms and furniture, refined and elegant colours in stuffs and porcelains, and subtlety of ornament in painting and *objets d'art*, that we think of as the ultimate *goût Français*.

For all her brilliance and inspiration, Jeanne de Pompadour has to be treated simply as a supremely gifted amateur. It was to take another woman, a century later, to change the status of decoration for ever. One of the lesser-known of the famous epigrams with which Elsie Mendl used to adorn her sofa-pillows was 'It takes a stout heart to live without roots'. As Lady Mendl, American born but European influenced, is now generally credited with having invented the profession of commercial interior decoration, these words have a special significance.

Lady Mendl knew what she meant by roots. She was not implying that your house must immediately impart the information that you were born at Blenheim, or Biloxi: for roots, in the sense of nostalgic bygones, can lead to much fuddy-duddiness in taste. Roots, for her, were more like branches, the strong long-lived timbers of beautiful proportion and shape and colour on which to hang the gilded leaves of decoration. These roots appeared time and again in the houses she decorated for clients and herself, as did her inventions – most memorably, shallow comfortable sofas and low tables, monochrome colours and mirrored, horizontal surfaces. Elsie Mendl certainly had a stout heart; for which read courage. Before her, no one had ever said 'I will pay you to decorate my house completely', which takes courage, too, on the part of the speaker. After her, almost no designer-decorated house has been devoid of her influence.

The exceptions to the Mendl-moulded future are few, but highly important. Another American, married into England, was to create what we now think of as the 'English style'. Nancy Lancaster's own yellow library and soft blue bedroom are pictured here and, though created only thirty years ago (and now lamentably destroyed), are the apogee of her style – a cool and eclectic view of the seventeenth and eighteenth centuries, rejecting anything ponderous, recreating an image of the past that is not in any way 'period', with all the tiresome historicism that word implies.

The nineteenth century has been the territory of the French genius Madeleine Castaing, who has carefully observed its tassels and bright colours, its quaintly shaped furniture, its fringes, its fantasy. The *haut-bourgeoisie* of the last-century Russia, Naples and Denmark, and the high-style of Austrian and French Rothschilds, have been her preferred *métiers*. Her work has the quality of rooms remembered from dreams, or imagined while reading novels. Hers is the taste of retrospection.

I assume that almost everyone has now outgrown the archaic picture, that, when given the go-ahead, decorators simply appear, clap their hands and say 'I see the whole thing in yellow satin' or whatever. Formerly, when decoration was simply a matter of re-doing existing rooms, this may often have been the case. Anything for a change. Many clients now find it is more satisfying to work with the designer from the start, and certainly the designer would rather have, and often now insists on, total control.

Decoration is a finely honed art, a discipline in which the client-designer balance must be carefully maintained. Museums are filled with exquisite, but needless, things, and it is necessary for the decorator to introduce the *petits soins* of everyday life, as well as the made-for-the-room Kent consoles, into his scheme. While the client may not, at first, appreciate the importance of this balance, lack of it will soon be apparent, as a bleak, unreal decor that nobody could live with.

Several of the rooms illustrated are the designers' own, some are created by the most brilliant non-professional decorators, but they all share the joyful exuberance of current designer-decoration, which knows no bounds in originality and fantasy. There are the new trends, the latest techniques, the aroma of nostalgia. This last is an ineradicable factor, for as long as there are buildings which still retain the aura of a vanished world, there will be people who wish to live and die within them. As more and more new structures are built, their inhabitants will want to decorate them in some personal way, and with luck there will be many more, and even better, decorated rooms. But, however beautiful the decorators make these rooms, there are two ingredients they cannot supply – interest in, and love of, the things in them, and the will to perpetuate. As Mario Praz has written, 'The Interior is the refuge of art. The true inhabitant is the collector. He takes it upon himself to transfigure things: to remove from objects, by possessing them, their quality of merchandise, the designer-decorated house is just such a refuge.

HISTORIC CHAMBERS FOR A TRAVELLING MAN

By opening an arch between the two rooms of a Regency apartment, Tom Parr, chairman of Colefax and Fowler, has created an elegant, comfortable London *pied-à-terre* for a modern gentleman which is also large enough to entertain forty people.

Albany, in Piccadilly, was turned from a family mansion into sets of exclusive chambers for gentlemen by the Duke of York and Albany in 1803. The apartments originally had no kitchens – the occupants would have sent out to a nearby restaurant for their food. Now there is a compact kitchen fitted in beside the hall.

Although he has given the apartment a rich Regency atmosphere, Tom Parr has

also borrowed ideas from the eighteenth century – such as the off-black skirting (base) boards – and used Victorian chintzes and specially built furniture. The mahogany doors which open flat back against the wall have been so carefully made that all the brass screws in the hinges are vertically aligned. There are several remembrances of his firm's founder, John Fowler, including the trefoil-shaped stool, covered in velvet with a deep, thickly tasselled fringe, and a carpet design, 'Rocksavage', discovered by Fowler at Cholmondeley Castle.

Overlooked by Robert Home's portrait of 'The King of Oudh', one of a collection of paintings by English artists in India and the Orient, is a mighty sofa, made to order and covered in rich green *velours de lin*, which doubles as the bed.

THE ENRICHING EFFECT OF A TAPESTRY

Anouska Hempel has created an atmosphere of age and opulence in this drawing room, in spite of its modern furniture and Oriental objects. The key to the richness is a single piece – an antique tapestry – which pulls together the colours and pale wood tones used in the room. The air of luxury is reinforced by the generous weight of the curtains – corded grey cotton, like the sofa – the dramatic use of carefully directed light, and the white marble floor inset with timber strips which unifies the whole ground floor of the house. A broad border stencilled beneath the drawing room cornice is echoed by a narrower border in the hall, framing the dining room door.

'BUTTAH-YELLAH' FOR A LEGENDARY TASTE MAKER

Overleaf Virginian-born Nancy Lancaster is the doyenne of English decorators. Thirty years ago she made this room, once the drawing office of the architect Wyatville, into her library, creating a model of the 'English Style'. Grand pieces – eighteenth-century pictures in ornate frames by William Kent, carved and gilded wall sconces, gilt Louis XVI chairs – are combined with comfortable cotton-covered sofas and armchairs. Glazed, varnished walls and unlined silk taffeta curtains radiate with colour. Mirrors around the door lighten and lengthen the room. *Trompe-l'oeil* swags at the end of the room were painted by John Fowler and George Oakes.

THREE MUCH-PATTERNED WELCOMING ROOMS

One bold chintz has been used for curtains, walls and upholstery in this welcoming room, *above*, but Mark Hampton has contained the bunches of roses by his use of touches of red. A collection of Victorian prints hang in strong red frames and the room itself is bound by a band of red braid. There are many soothing elements – humble coconut matting, one plain armchair and unadorned paintwork. In a converted church, *top right*, Nicholas Haslam has created a cunning piece of *trompe-l'oeil* as shutters of false books mimic the bookcase between the windows. There is a judicious mix of pattern and architectural features: the Turkey carpet covering the seat-cumtable, and different fabrics in green, yellow and white are blended with exaggerated

Gothic arches, a Chinese-Chippendale radiator grille and a spiral staircase. In another house, *below right*, plain curtains, a small scale pattern on the walls, and mahogany doors keep in check the plethora of pinks and reds and the almost riotous mixture of patterns on the upholstery.

COOL AND SUMPTUOUS
SPANISH DRAWING ROOM

Overleaf Symmetry is the key to the drawing room of this Marbella house, with furniture in pairs creating a formal sense of calm and balance. Spanish decorator Jaime Parlade has used cool colours and textures: white marble and terracotta floor, cream linen curtains glowingly lined in pink, Indian ivory, kilim-covered cushions, and an unusual use of crewelwork as tablecloths and for upholstery on a chair. Pink piping pulls the whole scheme together.

DINING ROOMS WITH WALLS AND SURFACES TO WATCH

Every surface has been painted in the dining room of an East Anglian house, *top*. The *faux marbre* panelled walls are painted in three shades; the table top is also painted like

marble; for relief, the rush-seated chairs are red, carefully edged with a fine white line. At the exact centre of each wall panel hangs a calendar print by Rex Whistler, framed, like the chairs, in red and white. *Below left* David Hicks has combined a carpet of his own design, geometrically patterned in two

shades of stone, with cream-painted chairs, copies of an eighteenth-century original. Their turquoise covers reflect the duck-egg blue framing the panelling, painted *en grisaille* in silver and pale blue. *Right* With consummate stagecraft, Parisian decorator François Catroux has framed the door

between his dining room and sitting room with white linen curtains. The dining chairs are draped in loosely made slip-covers of the same fabric. Surface textures are not all that they seem: the inlaid marble floor is in fact a patterned carpet laid in a classical, geometric floor pattern.

A FRENCH DINING ROOM WITH RUSSIAN OVERTONES

Overleaf The Parisian decorator Madeleine Castaing helped to create this dreamlike, aqueous dining room in the neo-classical Château de Vauboyen with its Russian-born owner. The winter-garden effect is achieved by filtering the daylight on to *eau-de-Nil* walls through curtains of transparent Indian silk, lined with turquoise. The doors have *trompe-l'oeil* panelling. Two small Biedermeier tables make a lighter and more intimate effect than one large one.

CURTAINS AND COLOURS
MAKE THE IMPACT

A delicate, quintessentially French, dining room has been created by an American in a Kensington villa, *top*. Its airy freshness contrasts with the gilded grandeur of a much smaller dining room, *below*, where cotton curtains in a broad green stripe are topped with a padded, gold-fringed pelmet. In a genuinely French, *fin-de-siècle* apartment, *right*, the opulence of the silk blinds and gilded wooden cornice is balanced by the austere elegance of the furniture.

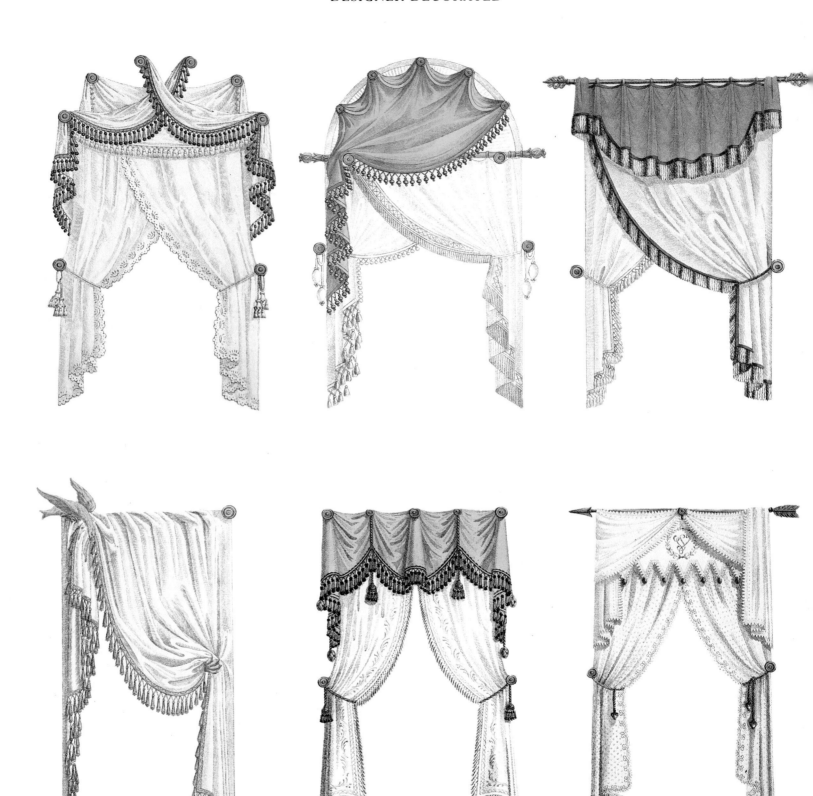

A FROTH OF COTTON AND SILK DRAPED BY INSPIRED HANDS

Most of these delicious confections for swagged, fringed and braided drapes and pelmets, based on designs by the Parisian upholsterer d'Hallevant, were published be-tween 1802 and 1835 by the influential fashion journalist Pierre de la Mésangère in *Meubles et Objets de Goût*, in *cahiers* of prints aimed at upholsterers and their clients. Many were then swiftly copied by Rudolf Ackermann in his periodical *The Repository of Art*, which was published in London. Such periodicals helped enormously to popularize the new Empire style, with its flamboyance and unashamed luxury. Napoleon and his Empress Josephine ordered quantities of drapes for the Royal palaces, fanning the enthusiasm of the Parisians for elaborate window dressings. These ideas are still an

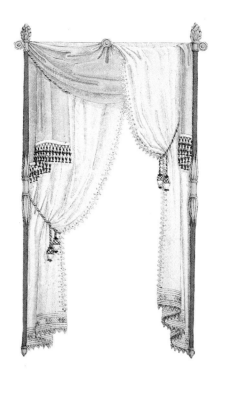

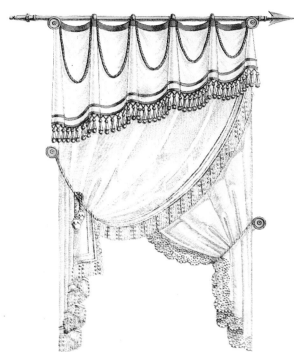

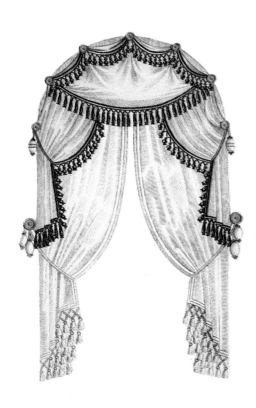

inspiration for decorators and can easily be adapted to any budget or style of interior. Some designs are complicated, and require special patterns (see *Practical Drapery Cutting* by E. Noetzli, 1906, reprinted by Potterton Books), but most of the best effects happen naturally as the fabric drapes itself. Any

fabric will work, as long as it falls in folds: silks, muslins, broderie anglaise, even fine wools can all be used. It is rewarding to experiment with translucent or heavier stuffs; with coloured linings and under-curtains; with contrasting colours of fabrics, and stripes or even patterns; with different

fringes, tassels, borders and tie-backs; and search out unusual rods. Drapes can be twined around a simple pole to create an unusual pelmet, and asymmetrical effects and unevenly sloping folds and tails can often soften a square window or disguise an unattractive view beyond.

AN ENTERTAINING AND EXOTIC DRAWING ROOM

In a London flat created for an Indian noblewoman, Nicholas Haslam has suffused the drawing room with unabashed exotica. The walls are curtained in raw silk bordered by a richly coloured wool fringe. The Aubusson carpet was copied from one made for Stanislas, an eighteenth-century king of Poland. Cushions made from precious antique silks and velvets are piled on a pair of white sofas, and the silver and blue fabric covering the cushion on the X-frame stool was made by Fortuny in Venice. A copy of a Gainsborough hangs above the drinks table. The window pelmet is an asymmetrical concoction of sheer white cotton, swagged and rosetted. Beneath it, the windows are screened by green slatted wood blinds with scarlet stringing.

There are no fewer than four separate seating areas in this room, making it ideal for large gatherings. For dinner parties, the table in the foreground, which has an extra leaf, pulls out to seat ten people. When not in use it sits unobtrusively behind the sofa.

THREE YELLOWS FOR A COUNTRY DRAWING ROOM

Overleaf Fire gutted this elegant drawing room in West Green House in 1982, but it has now been restored to its eighteenth-century glory with only antique cloths hiding the scarred tables as a reminder of the disaster. The most is made of a few grand pieces – a Chinese-Chippendale mirror, black and gold japanned chairs, an Aubusson rug and some blue and white Chinese vases. Three different shades of yellow on the panelling complement the soft English light and enhance the gilt, while a quite modest blue and white striped fabric on the armchairs reflects the colours of the porcelain. Bay trees with unusual split stems flank the fireplace.

MELLOW FELT WALLS IN A MASCULINE STUDY

This warm cocoon of a room is a banker's study in London. Anouska Hempel created it as a room to work in by lamplight, where there are no primary colours and rattan blinds filter the daylight. A dramatic spotlight falls on a nineteenth-century Japanese painting. Further Japanese elements are picked up in the red felt walls and curtains and the colours of the lacquer bowls upon the desk – their glossy surfaces echoed by the black shades of the converted oil lamps. The carpet, the same shade as the walls, also has a wide black border. The overall effect is warmly antique without deliberate attention to a particular period and the unobtrusive masculinity of the scheme works well.

STRONG COLOURS FOR A VIVID WOMAN

Tricia Guild, of Designers Guild, loves exuberant colours in her Chelsea home. Her palette is a vibrant mix of green, yellow and blue, and she has an artist's eye for juxtaposition and contrast. Here, an expensive French lemon silk brocade, more often used on unyielding formal furniture, covers a plump and comfortable easy chair. An ultra-modern Italian Memphis glass vase sits beside an Ivo Mosley dish on a Victorian tôle tray. The walls glow like a blackbird's egg behind the antique chest of drawers. Yet despite the absence of warm tones, the room is full of light, confirming the designer's view that with colour, if you use enough, everything works.

PERFECT GEOMETRY TO
PATTERN A FLOOR

Anthony Collett, formerly a sculptor, now an architect and decorator, has skilfully married several very disparate elements (an umbrella lamp, an Aesthetic Movement

glazed bookcase, a painting by Gilbert and George), blanked out the windows with white cotton blinds, and stripped and stained floorboards to create a strong and geometric interior, *top*.

John Stefanidis has applied similar restraint and attention to detail in a hallway,

below, to make an unassuming space seem luxurious. The shiny painted floor is copied from one in a Neapolitan palace, a bracketed shelf hides the radiator, the lanterns throw the light down on to the floor, and the panelling and cornice are impeccably finished for a simple backdrop.

AN ORIGINAL HOUSE
FIT FOR A MUSICAL GENIUS

'The Belvedere' at Montfort l'Amaury, out-side Paris, was the home of the composer Maurice Ravel from 1920 until his death in 1937. Ravel, a solitary, melancholy man,

took a close interest in its decoration. He was only five foot three inches tall, and the rooms – small in themselves – are furnished to complement his stature. The chequered floor is, daringly for its period, wall-to-wall carpeting, while the wallpaper is hand-painted, grey on grey, subtly softening the

strict geometry of the stripes. The straight lines are balanced by an abundance of curves in the furniture and even in the walls of the alcove. Ravel used black extensively throughout the house, although here it is subtly warmed by many different shades of grey varying from olive to dove.

INVENTIVE PAINT FINISHES IN A LONDON FLAT

Previous page Decorator Anthony Collett and painter David Champion have taken a traditional drawing room and treated it to an unconventional series of carpentry and paint effects. A massive architectural pediment over a mirror (the base conceals a radiator) gives the room – which is drawing room, dining room, bedroom and child's playroom – an air of theatrical grandeur. This is emphasized by the plywood pelmets around the bay window, intricately cut out, painted, then sponged over to subdue the yellow, black and white.

The windows are hung with fine chintz painted with the story of the Greek gods Phoebus and Boreas.

The surface textures make the room particularly distinctive. On the floor is a canvas rug painted by David Champion in the manner of crazy paving and then varnished so that it gleams and can be washed. The walls are plaster, painted with black-tinted size, topped by a pale wash and then scored and sanded to give an effect of graffiti. All the furniture except the brass table is painted; white chairs have been flicked with black paint and a Louis XVI-style armchair now resembles stone. The sofa ends are specially cut fretwork.

PERFECT DETAIL IN AN ENGLISH COUNTRY BEDROOM

A mark of David Mlinaric's style is his seemingly effortless attention to detail, demonstrated in one of the main bedrooms of a diminutive Palladian lodge. The fact that the day-bed, for example, is the exact width of the iron bedstead, or that an ebonized mirror-frame, *left*, has been found to match the Morris & Co. 'Sussex' armchair is no coincidence. The quality and finish of the paintwork, and the delicate stencilled frieze serve to emphasize the original details of the room, while the blue and white Chinese vase adds richness.

CHAIRS IN WHIRLS OF SKIRTS, FRILLS AND BOWS

Dressing up chairs is fun and adds elements of either grandeur or decidedly feminine chic to a room. The idea of covering dull tables with pretty cloths can be extended to chairs to give a dining room a party feel, or turn an unmatched group into a set. In this room, *left*, a dozen comfortable, low seats make the room look like a débutante ball, but are sufficiently narrow to fit tightly around the table, or round the walls, when

not in use. Two different patterned fabrics – checks and stripes – both piped with pink, ensure variety, while the bows give the covers a delightful party-dress look.

Simple striped cottons are equally effective on the most unpretentious chairs, *above*, which can be dressed up with skirts, bustles, pleats and bows. The notion has a respectable history: a Biedermeier-style birchwood chair has been draped with white cotton, trimmed with blue, copied from an original Biedermeier design by Josef Danhauser in 1820.

PEACE AND QUIET IN THE HEART OF LONDON

Nancy Lancaster's bedroom, now part of Colefax and Fowler's Brook Street show-rooms, was almost as much a living room as a place to sleep. The bed is treated simply, with a relatively austere couronne. Chintz curtains in an elegant blue shadow-ribbon design surround the windows looking out on to one of London's secret gardens. They match the fake panelling, painted by John Fowler in three shades of blue with white, complete with *faux* shadows.

A SETTING FIT FOR A STATELY FOUR-POSTER

An extra tall, eighteenth-century four-poster bed, surmounted by a painted blue and gold tester curved like the prow of a small ship, dominates this richly decorated master bedroom in a family house. Although the work of an amateur, with professional help, it is an immaculate attention to detail that creates the air of sheer luxury. The graduated hemline of the bed's gathered pelmet accentuates the curve of the tester and is finished with a

double layer of frills, one plain, the other striped taffeta. The window pelmet is trimmed with the same frilling, and its slightly uneven draping is much more pleasing than rigid perfection would be.

This is a light, relaxing room, despite being full of both plain and patterned colour – blue, green, red and cream in the Brussels carpet, the ribbon-and-flowers wallpaper, and the chaise covered in ribbon chintz (evidence that a patterned fabric can be buttoned successfully). Strong red squares on the patchwork bedcover are an essential touch in such a feminine room.

A PRISTINE BED IN A DEEP WINDOW ALCOVE

Nothing jars the senses in the white bedroom of illustrator Sue Curtis. The bed is framed by cream calico curtains in the window alcove, black and white filigree print fabric covers both cushions and shutters, and the white canvas floor is regularly renewed to preserve its pristine whiteness. The unusual vase on the floor comes from a glove-shop display.

LACY FRETWORK FOR CUPBOARD DOORS

Anthony Collett's uncluttered bedroom, with its simple rush matting and walls of grey-smudged parchment white, is enlivened by the shamelessly decorative wardrobe, cut to his own design. Generous architectural features, such as the deep mouldings, ensure that the effect is not austere. Friends each embroidered one square of the bedcover as a wedding gift.

ENDLESS DESERT VIEWS IN A COTTAGE BEDROOM

Overleaf The view from the pop-star Adam Ant's silk-tented bed is a *trompe-l'oeil* vista of the Egyptian desert created by Dominic Bon de Sousa and painters Peter Sheldon and Rashid Topham. It is hard to see where the real shimmering silk of the tent ends and the painted version begins. A painted sword leans against the tent pole but its guard is really the doorhandle.

WELL-DRESSED BEDS

1 The look of an Elizabethan manor has been achieved in a Victorian terrace house. 2 A bed festooned in cream and ivory silk is spread with antique lace. 3 Anouska Hempel has displayed a collection of shell pictures within a bed generously hung with heavy, natural cotton. 4 Panelled walls and furniture are stencilled with ferns to match the chintz. 5 In Marbella, a traditional French *toile de Jouy* covers everything. 6 Tricia Guild gave this blue bedroom quilted hangings. The tablecloth has a heavy rouleau hem. 7 *Trompe-l'oeil* and real silk

7

8

9

10

11

12

hangings have been combined to create a bed in a fantastical Napoleonic campaign tent. 8 A rusticated carved wooden bed is hung *à la Polonaise* in blue wild silk against walls of plum, blue and sage cotton.

9 Milliner David Shilling drapes muslin over a French boulle bed. The light is concealed inside the couronne. 10 In the French style, every surface is covered with one highly patterned fabric; even the prints

on the wall are of Sèvres china. 11 Anthony Collett designed his own ebony and sycamore bed, hung with raw silk. 12 A big, Arts and Crafts-style bed still leaves plenty of space in a small room.

GILDED STAIRWAY TO ANCIENT EGYPTIAN MYSTERY

A carpeted staircase leading to a hidden bedroom was painted by Peter Sheldon and Rashid Topham to resemble an ancient Egyptian temple, complete with a message to their pop-star client in pseudo-hieroglyphics on the large pillar. The *trompe-l'oeil*, which includes dramatic shafts of light that strike the lotus-leafed column, extends into reality; one arrow placed casually against the crumbling wall is real, one is illusion. The painted and gilded staircase has been distressed to give the appearance of age and complement the backdrop.

EXUBERANT CLASSICISM IN A PARIS APARTMENT

Geoffrey Bennison, renowned for his originality, imaginative taste and inexhaustible knowledge, gave the square, high hallway of this eighteenth-century Paris apartment a wonderfully baroque treatment, with a pair

of extravagantly painted marbled doors surmounted by a *trompe-l'oeil* relief of garlanded putti. Seventeenth-century copies of Imperial Roman busts stare down impassively, while black porphyry crowns the tall column by the doors. Everything has been artificially aged, including the ornately trimmed faded pink curtains.

GLITTERING NOCTURNAL MAGNIFICENCE

Overleaf Confronted with a set of dark, north-facing rooms, Geoffrey Bennison chose to exclude all the natural light, introducing instead the glitter of the night. In the dining room – which may once have been a ballroom – he has created a perfect marriage of grandeur and frivolity. Rows of blue and white Chinese vases contrast with the gilded splendour of mirrors and gilt party chairs beneath a flickering, candlelit chandelier. A small table adds intimacy and enchantment where a larger one could have spoilt the magical effect.

MINIMAL

Balance, restraint and self-discipline characterize the
minimal style whether it appears in an almost empty concrete loft
or a refined London flat stripped of all but a few objects.
This is the approach of many architects and designers who follow,
or form, the latest trends with a single-minded commitment. Their
homes may have been created in old buildings or modern steel
and glass structures, but they are always showcases for
contemporary taste and awareness. The rooms are devoid of
mess: all the trappings of everyday life regarded as unsuitable for
show are hidden away – each interior has been edited to the
smallest detail of perfection.

Narrow slatted venetian blinds filter the light from one of several
tall windows in a 1930s apartment block in the centre of Brussels. With white walls,
a modern *chaise longue* covered in white cotton, and fine black heating-grilles in the floor,
the effect is as theatrical as the illuminated art deco plaster mask.

hen is the rest of the furniture coming? If you live in a minimalist interior you will be asked this question repeatedly. Rooms without traditional reference points or visual diversions seem to unsettle and perplex people. The kind of terms used to describe minimalist spaces – stark, austere, spartan, puritanical – reveal a certain distrust of what appears, on the surface, to be quite uncomfortable to live in.

In the West we are visually overstimulated, bombarded with information and conditioned to believe in achievement, goals and results. Zen philosophy, one source of inspiration for minimalism, says that each moment is as important as the next, that end-gaining is fruitless. The prize is stillness and simplicity.

Another source of inspiration are the rationalist architects from the Greeks to Palladio to Le Corbusier, whose concern with proportion, harmony and balance dictated interior spaces. Le Corbusier, in particular, found beauty in function and believed that the design of a space should arise primarily out of the needs of the individuals who use it. In a modern, urban age, these needs are for air, light and labour-free working conditions. Corbusier's declaration that the house is a 'machine for living in' has been denigrated as a recipe for brutality when he was really expressing a belief that architecture could actually provide a better way of life.

A minimalist interior is a space in which you see everything clearly: people, colours, surfaces and form. Every object, even the simplest, becomes important. The concept of choosing to live with the minimum is generally anathema to Westerners, who are brought up to acquire and consume compulsively. In the cities of Japan, where square footage is at a premium, there is a true appreciation of empty space. In a Japanese home, a single flower will be displayed where we would have a bunch, or a single picture will be hung on the wall instead of several. In time, the single picture may well be taken down and replaced by another, but the Japanese prefer knowing one thing well to surrounding themselves with an array of objects all competing for attention.

A minimalist interior also reveals bad workmanship, poor materials and awkward design: it is unforgiving of mistakes. For this reason, minimalism is not cheap. Surfaces must be flawless, details precise, and every object well-designed, all of which costs money. It also takes dedication and persistence to meet such standards: contractors, for example, will tell you that it is 'not standard building practice' to do without skirting boards.

Such living demands rigorous planning beforehand and stern vigilance afterwards. Even when you are prepared to pare down your possessions to the most basic level, there still must be places to put essentials – books, food, clothes – which means building cupboards so unobtrusively you hardly know they are there. Neatness, cleanliness and scrupulous maintenance are required. Dirt shows up on vast open surfaces and so do cracks in the plaster, marks on the paintwork and stains on the carpet. You cannot shove dirty clothes under the bed, or hide an overflowing waste-paper basket behind the drapes when friends drop in. And, as yet, nobody has solved the noise problem. Hard surfaces and near-empty rooms amplify sound uncomfortably.

However much time and effort it takes, minimalist living has its rewards. Objects are chosen for a purpose – there is a freedom from the tyranny of knick-knacks, or what my mother used to call 'dustcatchers'. Everything has its own place. There is no concern with changing fashion, colour schemes, or styles of room arrangement. Instead you are forced to pay attention to what is elemental – the quality of light, form and proportion. Being so profligate with space gives rise to a positive feeling of exhilaration. Perhaps the greatest defence of the minimal interior is that it does not dictate what you put in it providing the pieces that you choose are beautiful. A 'good' space will accommodate a fine Empire chair just as happily as a Corbusier *chaise longue*.

There are many versions of minimalism and some are more minimal than others. My own spaces stop short of absolute bareness, and my appropriation of Zen ideas of architecture would seem sloppy to an Easterner. But whatever attitude is being expressed, these quiet enclaves are an attempt to come to terms with the frenzy and stress of urban life.

The key to minimalism is exposure. It is the lack of camouflage, visual distraction and disguise that make some people uneasy about these spaces. Once experienced, however, life without conventional props proves to be soothing and serene. Pure space, filled with thoughts rather than things, is good for the soul.

1

2

3

4

LIVING IN A COLOURFUL MEXICAN MASTERPIECE

The celebrated Mexican architect, Luis Barragán, came out of semi-retirement to build this small private house in Mexico City. Vibrant colour, painstaking composition, the play of sunlight and shadow on bare walls and, especially, on water are his trademarks. He cites as his inspiration the

quiet courtyards of religious buildings in both Mexico and Spain and the colourful life of rural villages. He spent a year studying under Le Corbusier in Paris in the 1930s, but in his own work he has gone beyond functionalism, stressing that his buildings are for the emotional realities of life, for refuge from the modern world.

He uses the language of abstraction to great effect, so that objects as simple as

potted cacti, framed by lavender walls (4), assume the status of a piece of sculpture. Colour and composition are constantly changed by the sunlight. The door leading off the patio (1) is deliberately small to mislead the eye and give an impression of larger scale and greater space.

The owners of this house approached Barragán in 1976 and asked him to build a small home with an integral swimming pool.

5

6

7

8

After considering the commission for six months, the master said yes. The result is three rectangular units around a patio (one housing the pool), where the plays on perspective are endless, and abstract planes change constantly as sunlight, filtered through whitewashed windows, moves around walls and water. The light reflected diagonally off the water highlights his striking use of colour and adds life to an otherwise contemplative structure. A vivid crimson pillar (6) dives into the pool, overlooked by the dining room where a solid pine table sits on polished flagstones (7). There are other rooms which, by necessity, require beds, chairs and other paraphernalia, but these spacious, inward-looking yards and passages are the essence of the house – an oasis amid the city.

The theme of escape is vital: Barragán wanted every window whitewashed or painted, blocking out the world outside. In the broad passage from entrance to pool (5 and 8), for instance, the glass is painted yellow. And if Barragán sees his architecture as art, then those who live in a masterpiece also have their obligations: the owners of this house employ a full-time painter and odd-job man to counteract the effects of pollution on the work of art they inhabit.

EMPTY ROOMS LINED WITH FULL CUPBOARDS

Architect John Pawson has solved the problem of clutter. He does not mind possessions – they are all there, crammed into cupboards – but he prefers not to have them on show around him. His solution is to reduce the number of pieces of furniture, books, ornaments, pictures and utensils to an absolute minimum, preferring visual comfort to physical convenience. The kitchen is empty of cups, pans, wooden spoons, or even a plug for the moulded steel sink; plumbing, wiring and lighting are all hidden away. And although a five-year-old child is allowed to play with her toys between school and bedtime, when she is out or asleep you would never suspect her existence. Some essentials of both life and architecture remain, and these are turned

into virtues. Skirting (base) boards have disappeared, but the fireplace and the cornice have been allowed to stay.

Some furniture has to be tolerated, and what cannot be rolled up and stowed away by day, like the black Japanese futons, is classic in design. A Dimplex heater tries to

look unobtrusive and the television has been built into the wall, surrounded by those essential white-lacquered cupboards. Even paintings are stored there, then taken out, two at a time, and leant against the walls rather than hung, just in case a feeling of permanence should ensue. Used for dining

sleep, work and play, the main room is an empty stage on which the normal daily activities are acted out, with the appropriate props ceremoniously produced from cupboards to set the scenes. And, when you stop thinking about what is *not* there, you realize that rooms can be nice without things.

AN IVORY TOWER
IN A SURPRISING SETTING

Set into the steeply gabled roof of an imposing nineteenth-century Flemish villa, this dramatic triangular window is a recent addition to the home of an antique dealer. It has turned the attic into a contemporary ivory tower that comes as a surprising conclusion to the otherwise traditionally furnished building. The objects are all modern treasures: a prowling terracotta panther is signed 'Bugatti', the glass table set on industrial castors is by Gae Aulenti, the Torso chair was designed by Paolo Deganello for Cassani. But not everything is what it seems – tall columns flanking the silent organ pipes are hi-fi speakers.

MODERN FURNITURE
AS ABSTRACT COMPOSITION

The underlying architecture of an early twentieth-century Brussels flat, neutralized by white paint, provides an unobtrusive frame for the careful selection of colours and objects. Decorator Barbara Stoeltie arranged the sculptural pieces in her drawing room to stand so graphically in relation to each other that they hardly seem like furniture. The geometric rug was designed by René Stoeltie and one of his paintings hangs over the red 1920s Chippendale-style table. Although the elements of the room are kept to the minimum, the perfection of each piece generates an overall feeling of highly discriminate luxury.

WHERE UPRIGHTS ARE
A LAW UNTO THEMSELVES

Anarchy reigns in a pop-guitarist's London flat. The interior of an Edwardian mansion block has been transformed by architect David Connor and painter Madelaine Palme into an area of conflicting perspectives and crazed murals. The sloping skirting board and door-frame completely disguise the upright outline of the actual door, and the painted triangular table ensures that there is no right angle in sight.

UNREGIMENTED SPACE IN
BLACK AND WHITE

The owners of this penthouse flat in a warehouse overlooking the City of London raised a family in a rambling suburban house. Alone at last, they commissioned architect Simon Condor to build them a space of their very own.

Starting with one enormous floor area, rooms have been created without corridors or doors and without losing that all-important sense of space. The curved walls,

which do not all reach the ceiling, block the view from one living area to another, but do not prevent the light from the perimeter windows reaching the centre of the floor. Concealed strip lighting at floor level emphasizes the curved black shelving and tops up the natural light. Black carpeting unites the different areas, which are sparsely furnished with design classics. Built-in furniture, such as the cylindrical drinks and hi-fi cupboard, is also curved. The radiators are recessed and slim white pillars add structural support.

AN ARRANGEMENT OF HIGHLY UNLIKELY OBJECTS

A touch of drama, however temporary, is always worth striving for. Two ensembles have been put together to show the kinds of theatrical effects that can be easily achieved by combining fragile objects with rough-and-ready raw materials not usually considered for decorative displays.

The exuberant grey and blue paintwork, *previous page*, was dashed on to the wall to pick up the deep blues and blacks of some of the objects on the table. A graceful, Hammerite-finish, metal console table bears an assortment of dishes, and glass pieces, made by Anna Dickinson, which combine etched glass with copper rims,

and wire threaded with seed pearls and twined with gold thread. Wire wool fills a marble and stone bowl, seaweed and wooden spills grace other vessels: given the right combination, even these apparently mundane materials take on rare qualities.

In what might be an abandoned Roman villa, *above*, another glass-topped metal table, finished with an oxidized bronze effect by designer Jean-Michel Wilmotte, bears more pieces by Anna Dickinson in glass and patinated-copper, sitting like amphorae from some lost Mediterranean trading vessel. The larger vases and the bowl on a bronze stand under the table, are Venetian glass. Autumn leaves, moss, and brambles encroach on the scene and verdigris encrusts the wall behind.

INSTANT ARCHAEOLOGY IN A LONDON DINING ROOM

The *enfant terrible* of the architectural establishment, Nigel Coates, has simply left a job half-done in order to achieve this effect in his South Kensington flat. A small central hall, flanked by grand double doors, has been turned into a square dining room.

He has added energy to the classical stability of the original architectural features, with a patchy concrete floor, simple curtains and half-stripped doors. The dining table has a round mirror at its centre, like a large jewel, and the 'dog' chairs, which fold up at a twitch of their leather tails, seem coiled ready to spring; they were made to his own design.

ARCHITECTURAL MOULDING IN A MUSIC ROOM

A monumental doorway of *faux* stone, with matching skirting board and console table, gives a feeling of classical antiquity in the music room of a concert pianist's small flat. The pediment above the door conceals a light to increase the sense of height, and the console table, crammed with modern ceramics, extends to become a dining table.

EXQUISITELY CONSIDERED CLASSICAL BARENESS

Minimalism does not have to mean modernism. Designer Peter Leonard combines an impressive chimney-piece and a campaign bed upholstered in mattress ticking (reversed for a more subdued stripe) with a glass and metal table of his own design against a shiny chestnut strip floor. The result is both rich and spare.

EAST MEETS WEST IN A PARIS APARTMENT

Oriental and European styles come together in the airy Paris drawing room, *overleaf*, of the Japanese fashion designer, Kenzo. The low table and bronze tiger, made for the 1855 Paris World Fair, are both Japanese. The *chaise longue* and a set of antique French chairs are upholstered in fabric from Thailand.

MODERN CRAFTSMANSHIP AND PERMANENCE

A newly constructed panelled rotunda, designed by the New York architect Lee Mindel, has created a core at the centre of a large Central Park West apartment. Instead of one unwieldy floor area, now there is defined space, and extra rooms have been created. Different coloured inlaid strips in the pale wooden floor lead the eye through the reorganized area, connecting room with room. Light, too, flows through the space, enhanced by six different shades of white paint. Built-in storage cupboards give the structure an architectural permanence and solidity, and all the joinery is of the highest craftsmanship – the rotunda itself is made from seventy separate sections.

NOW YOU SEE IT . . . NOW YOU DON'T

In a fashion designer's Greenwich Village house, the past literally intrudes into the present. The owner refers to the objects disappearing through the walls as 'illusionary memories'. In the entrance hall, a plaster-impregnated mackintosh hangs from a hook, and a riding crop and hat perch on the edge of a table. For their elegance and simplicity these surreal devices rival the decorative plasterwork of the eighteenth and nineteenth centuries, but they are also functional – in other rooms they conceal ducts and pipes for heating, air-conditioning and other modern needs. The effect is unmistakably contemporary yet stresses the continuity of the past with the present.

NEUTRAL SETTING
FOR ANTIQUE AND MODERN

After two years of searching for the essentially Venetian apartment, antique dealer Carlo Medioli found it – in a loft at the top of the fifteenth-century Ca' Bernardo. He then proceeded to excise all references to location or history, painting every surface pristine white and blocking out the views of rooftops, water and Venetian decay with perpetually drawn, grey taffeta curtains. Against this neutral background he has mixed antique with modern, relishing the freedom to be creative with old pieces in new and original combinations. Although he specializes professionally in the eighteenth century, the furnishings in his apartment are mostly neo-classical and art deco with a

theme of black and white, but virtually every period is represented. He composes striking groups of furniture that float in the seamless space, where floors disappear into walls and walls into ceilings.

Typical of his arrangements is a discreet sitting area, *above*, with French art nouveau sofa and chairs and a twelfth-century stone griffin. Beyond this, to the left, is a mid-1960s Castelli dining chair, which sits at an art deco dining table.

In the bedroom, he has mixed a modern Fortuny-style wall hanging, made by a friend, with a voluptuous French eighteenth-century day-bed by George Jacob, master craftsman to both Marie Antoinette and the Empress Josephine. Flanking the bed, a pair of cherrywood tables on curving swans' heads, are nineteenth-century Florentine.

CONCRETE STAIRCASE FLYING FREE IN ANTWERP

Previous page Two simple white sofas sit cosily around a television set in one corner of a vast industrial loft space in Antwerp. A narrow concrete staircase, designed by architect Kris Mys, floats effortlessly, defying its weight – a flying staircase from an eighteenth-century mansion could not be more theatrical. It cuts clean through the levels of the loft and divides the space, which otherwise has no need for walls. Spotless grey concrete and white paint are the only decoration in this exhilarating, totally unfettered space.

PLAIN WHITE TILES FOR TWO BATHROOMS

Walls of glass brick ensure privacy in a bathroom in the same Antwerp loft but allow the natural and artificial light to flood into the room. White tiles, from floor to ceiling, encase the room, and the proportions of every fitment are determined by the tiles, reducing everything to one coherent unit of measurement. This and the kitchen are the only 'rooms' in the loft, yet here, around bath and lavatory, walls exist within walls. Two factory lockers on the right hide toothbrushes, mirror and all other signs of organic life: convenience is

ruthlessly sacrificed to the concept of the space – even at life's most basic level.

The same idea has been used to very different effect in a new bathroom inspired by the work of the original architect of the house, the Belgian Louis de Koninck. Built in 1928, the house has a purity of design that still looks modern today. Walls, steps and platforms, all constructed of square white tiles, create a rectangular composition. Its ordered beauty is then successfully subverted by an ordinary curved washbasin, the curved lines of a tubular steel-and-glass table designed in the 1930s to hold medical instruments, and a conspicuously indulgent, richly decorated art deco vase.

ANCESTRAL

Generations of one family in the same house are reflected
in the ancestral style at its finest. It can be preserved, and copied
– at great expense – but the lives that required those vast
and numberless saloons of paintings and treasures have long
disappeared, leaving behind them a permanent memorial to an
age when money was spent without check, sometimes to
ruination. Tapestry, portraits, gilding, wall paintings, handwoven
carpets, handmade furniture – all the trappings of an ancestral
interior are essentially labour intensive. And with modern
inventions the endless rooms below stairs for those
who sustained the edifice, for maids, butlers, footmen, cooks
and scullery maids, are no longer needed.

A massive door, flanked by gilded decorative reliefs and
presided over by larger than life-size figures, leads from the magnificent Double
Cube room to the Great Antechamber at Wilton House, near Salisbury. The cartouche
above the door is quartered with the Herbert family arms.

When I was a boy of about nine or ten, my parents took me to Wilton for the first time. The brief visit, like others which followed, was not an occasion when I felt particularly welcome or at ease. My grandmother, a formidable woman, frightened me; even more terrifying was walking through the cloisters, with its array of stone statues leering out of the gloom. At night I would steel myself to run flat out from one end to the other, convinced that arms would reach out to grab me.

The state apartments and the Double Cube room do not figure large in these first impressions – small boys rarely take account of fine detailing and noble proportions. But I do remember that the rest of the house was unbelievably sombre. What was not painted dark green – my grandmother's favourite colour – was dark brown. The library, then as now the family drawing room, was encased in panelling and lined with books. The atmosphere was relentlessly Victorian.

Wilton is a square house with a hollow centre. Part of it is Tudor, part Inigo Jones, part Wyatt; the elements blend comfortably, testifying to the skill with which succeeding generations have altered, improved and restored. In 1601 my ancestor complained: 'I have not yet been a day in the country and I am as weary of it as if I had been a prisoner there seven years'. It is hard to understand why he should have been so bored – at the time he wrote, Wilton was renowned as a centre of learning and of the arts. The first performance of Shakespeare's *As You Like It* is said to have taken place in a formal garden south of the house. Later, at the instigation of Charles I, Inigo Jones was commissioned to replan the house so that it would be suitable for entertaining royalty.

During the nineteenth century and up to the Second World War, Wilton functioned as a typical country house. House parties of politicians and ambassadors – about twenty at a time – came for extended weekend visits of four days or more. In Victorian times, gentlemen stayed in Bachelor's Row, a long corridor of rooms on the ground floor, some prohibitive distance from Maiden Lane upstairs, where the ladies were accommodated. Sexes were equally segregated below stairs. One family photograph, dating from about 1870, shows a fierce housekeeper, bristling with bunches of keys, looking more like a gaoler than the supervisor of the female staff. Children lived in the North-West Tower, which was known as the Nursery Tower; periodically they were brought down, admired and then sent back again.

House-party pursuits can be surmised from the number of rooms devoted to specific purposes: the chapel, for Sunday worship; the library, for reading and letter writing; the smoking-room, with its connecting billiard room; and a number of anterooms, including the Cube room and hunting room, presumably places where people gathered before moving on somewhere else – to the Double Cube room for a reception, perhaps, or to the big dining room.

At the turn of the century there were more than thirty gardeners at Wilton and as many indoor staff; a household which required that there be staff to look after staff. At the lower level, the cloister connected service rooms: a huge kitchen, cellar, pantry, linen-room and dining hall for the servants. But there was no servants' wing, just a series of rooms scattered all over the house. The laundry was located in a separate building a quarter-mile from the house.

In 1950 Wilton opened to the public, one of the first stately homes to do so. More changes came about in 1960 when my father commissioned John Fowler, whom he greatly admired, to redecorate the family bedrooms, library and cloisters. Considering my grandmother's taste, almost any alteration would have been warmer and more welcoming. Fowler, with his bold ideas and brilliance at handling colour, particularly in understanding what big rooms could take, painted the cloisters apricot terracotta over a yellow ground; a treatment, which although not strictly speaking authentic, was nevertheless what John Cornforth has described as one of Fowler's 'triumphs of architectural painting'.

My father, who ran the estate for twenty five years and lived in the house for nine, probably knew Wilton better than anyone. One day he was astonished to discover a trapdoor in a room in the estate office. Underneath lay all the family papers, dating back to 1700. Knowing my father's thoroughness, I never expected to make any discoveries of my own, yet barely six months after my wife and I moved into the house, I opened a cupboard next to a staircase used a hundred times a day and found, beneath a quarter-inch of black dust, boxes of Victorian Christmas decorations; enormous thin glass globes, each with a pink, green or yellow ribbon for hanging on the tree. From the date on the newspapers lining the shelves it was clear that the cupboard had not been opened for fifty years although it was in plain view. We were delighted with our discovery; the decorations now hang on our tree every year.

Over the next five years, Wilton will undergo a programme of restoration, with the aim of making the house secure for the future. In five centuries, these are the first comprehensive repairs ever carried out. Work on the eighteenth-century Palladian bridge has already been completed; next on the agenda is the roof, followed by the tower which has sunk a few inches over the years. Inside, rooms will be tackled one by one, working anti-clockwise around the house.

The problem with restoration is deciding how far to go. In a purely practical sense, the budget limits how much can be done; it was not possible, for example, to replace every damaged stone in the bridge, just the worst ones. But the object is not to replace old with new, however authentically this can be accomplished. There would be nothing worse than ending up with the rooms looking as though they had just been finished. Like many ancestral homes, Wilton is the product of many generations of alteration, each layer subtly integrated with the others. That is at least part of the reason why it remains a house which is comfortable and easy to live in, not a relic of the past.

COLONIAL MEMENTOES IMPRESSIVELY MOUNTED

The interior of Clandeboye in County Down, Ulster, is a testament to the life, travels and good works of its illustrious former owner, the 1st Marquess of Dufferin and Ava (1806–1902), ambassador to France, Russia, Turkey and Italy, Governor-General of Canada and Viceroy of India.

Here in the Inner Hall the traditional baronial method of displaying armour and weapons on the walls has been adapted for Lord Dufferin's collection of trophies and mementoes: skis, paddles, brushes, lacrosse sticks, ice picks, snow shoes and tomahawks are hung in geometric patterns on chicken wire. A set of huge, well-used scarlet leather chairs and a sofa face each other in front of the log fire, separated by a grinning polar bear, forever flattened into submission on a Turkey carpet.

SPLENDID MODERNITY FOR A VICTORIAN MAGNATE

Only a great industrialist of the 1890s could have created Kinloch Castle. Sir George Bullough built his shooting lodge on the deserted Scottish island of Rhum and then staffed it with a hundred people, all for his annual visit of three weeks. He wanted all the trappings and grandeur of a stately home – in the double height hall, *above*, the 'Jacobean' panelling was carved *in situ* by forty joiners; sporting trophies line the walls and cover the floor – but he also insisted on the most up-to-date comforts possible. There was central heating, double glazing, an internal telephone exchange, a generator to keep the lamps twinkling above the ballroom floor, and the last word in plumbing. An extractor fan kept the smoking-room fresh, and beer and soda engines effervesced to quench the thirst.

VICTORIAN HERALDRY IN A MEDIEVAL HOUSE

Like many ancestral houses in Britain, the original medieval bones of Flintham, in Northamptonshire, have been fleshed out by successive generations. The Victorian incumbents faced the exterior with stone in the Italian palatial style, but fitted out the dining room in the heraldic fashion of the times. Dark wood panelling and candle sconces were built around the family portraits. The lamp suspended from the painted ceiling was once a gasolier. The original Victorian table and buttoned leather chairs were recently rescued from the attic, having been banished earlier this century in favour of Georgian furniture.

ONE OF THE FIRST SEPARATE DINING ROOMS IN FRANCE

All the furniture at the Château de Montgeoffroy on the Loire dates from the 1770s when the house was built for the Marquis de Contades, Maréchal of France. The oval dining room was one of the first to be built in France; before, the French had preferred to dine in their *salons*. The Marquis' chef invented pâté de foie gras, which may have first been served at this very table. Painted Louis XV chairs have extra wide seats to support the ladies' billowing skirts, and low backrests offer discreet support. The white ceramic stove, with a chimney in the shape of a palm tree, was a gift from the people of Strasbourg.

A SHIMMERING ROOM FOR CANDLELIT DINNERS

Overleaf Decorated in the early eighteenth century with magnificent plasterwork and tapestries, the Earl and Countess of Chichester's dining room is as grand as any in the land. The room is at its shimmering best by candlelight and so, in summer, when it is not dark until late, the daylight is blocked out by special panels fitted to the outside of the windows. Tawny pink walls are traditionally achieved by adding fresh pig's blood to matt white oil paint. The table is surrounded by painted Regency chairs and set with octagonal engraved glasses of Bohemian crystal, silver birds and candelabra entwined with flowers.

PALLADIAN SOPHISTICATION IN AN UNTAMED LANDSCAPE

Ebberston Hall, set amid wild Yorkshire countryside, is a lilliputian stately home designed by Colen Campbell in 1715 as a summer retreat and fishing lodge. All the rooms are proportioned according to Palladio's rules: the blue hall with diagonal paving is exactly twice as long as it is wide. The white-panelled dining room was once a loggia, with large windows through which to view the water gardens.

A QUARTET OF PUBLIC ROOMS ON PARADE

These four halls in England and Ireland, with furniture and sculpture marshalled around the edges and an extravagant waste of space, are clearly intended to impress. Each relies on a single colour for the walls, with white or shades of putty, stone and snuff for the wood and plasterwork.

The rococo hall at Burton Constable in Yorkshire, *top left*, dates from 1763. The owner, William Constable, made a point of

using local craftsmen to save money – the ceiling, by Henderson of York, cost £52 17s ½d. The Gothic cloister at Wilton House, *top right*, was remodelled in 1801 by James Wyatt to connect the celebrated classical rooms that surround it. Gothic detailing in the hall, *below left*, at Luttrellstown, outside Dublin, was added this century by Felix Harbord. At Newbridge, *below right*, also near Dublin, the Wedgwood blue, stone-flagged inner hall provides a moment of repose before the visitor enters the Great Red Drawing Room beyond.

FAMILY PORTRAITS
IN A MAGNIFICENT SETTING

The Double Cube room (60 × 30 × 30 feet) at Wilton House was designed in 1652 by Inigo Jones, expressly to house six of the Earl of Pembroke's family portraits by Van Dyck. The carved and gilded sofas and chairs, covered with crimson velvet, were designed a hundred years later by William Kent; the massive white and gold side tables are by Chippendale. At the far end of the room, beneath the largest Van Dyck, is a nineteenth-century sofa upholstered with patterned carpet from the Wilton factory.

The Double Cube connects with a suite of smaller, but equally magnificent, rooms. Impossible to heat, they must have been ideal for a brisk walk in the mornings, and the warmth of a thousand candles would transform them into the most perfect setting for evening receptions.

CHIPPENDALE FURNITURE
DESIGNED FOR THE ROOM

The drawing room at Aske, in Yorkshire, the seat of the Marquess of Zetland, is the very epitome of grand, country-house style: formal and yet also giving thought to comfort. The Marquess' forebear made his fortune as a draper in Edinburgh, supplying the British and Prussian armies during the Seven Years War. He then bought property

all over England, becoming a man of influence and a patron of the arts. The three sofas and four chairs covered in red damask are the remaining part of a unique set – the only furniture in existence known to have been made by Thomas Chippendale to designs by Robert Adam. The ceiling, glinting with the gold leaf used to pick out the plasterwork, is by Capability Brown, a designer more usually associated with the landscaping of parks.

TREASURE HOUSE CREATED BY A MAN IN EXILE

Overleaf Kingston Lacy was the creation of the wild and wilful William John Bankes, friend of Lord Byron, scholar, antiquarian and collector. He toiled ceaselessly but was never to see the transformation of his family seat into an Italianate palazzo because he fled the country in 1839 to avoid standing trial for indecency. He supervised the

renovations from abroad and from his yacht anchored off the Dorset coast, when delivering more treasures.

Since Bankes' day, the sun-drenched drawing room, with its dusky pink silk damask walls, has taken on a more feminine air. But it is still his collection of pictures that dominates; the smaller works are hung in close formation just above the chair rail, with larger portraits by Van Dyck and Romney higher up.

A GLITTERING SICILIAN MIRRORED BALLROOM

Palazzo Gangi is pure Sicilian baroque, hidden away in a network of tiny streets and piazzas in the heart of Palermo. Princess Stefanina Gangi watches over her inheritance with an eagle eye although she no longer lives there.

The Hall of Mirrors, with its Murano glass chandeliers hanging from a double-vaulted ceiling, is the triumphant conclusion to a walk through the blue, green and red rooms that precede it. On the walls, gilded mirrors are interspersed with painted panels ablaze with golden garlands, arabesques and serpentine decorations. The floor is painted majolica tilework. Concealed lighting was introduced by Luchino Visconti to illuminate the vaulting when he borrowed this room for ballroom scenes in his film *The Leopard*.

CONVIVIAL GROUPING IN A VICTORIAN ROOM

Brodsworth Hall in Yorkshire was built in the 1860s to a grand neo-classical design. The halls and passages, executed in marble and stone, are imposing, but the crimson and gold drawing room, *right*, is most cheerful. Glittering chandeliers, giant mirrors and Louis XVI furniture confirm the atmosphere of late-Victorian sociability.

A LIBRARY THAT HAS REGAINED ITS FORMER GLORY

The fire that gutted Sledmere House, York-shire, in 1911 was less of a disaster for the library than it might have been. All the original moulds for its magnificent plaster-work had been kept by the firm of Jacksons in London for just such a contingency. This 120-foot-long room is consequently an exact replica of the 1790 original. The present head of the Sykes family has added his own flamboyant stamp to the library with a ceiling, picked out in 24-carat gold leaf, that dances with glittering brilliance in the morning sun.

ROCOCO TRIUMPH BUILT FOR AN ABBOT

Any visitor to the library at Schussenried in southern Germany could be excused for feeling an urge to dance. The ballroom-like space is lined with pale blue and gold bookcases – their sybaritic curves and swirling arabesques seem to yearn for an orchestra and the rustle of silk. It is a superlative flowering of the rococo tech-nique, fusing architecture, sculpture, paint-ing and symbolism. Yet this enchanted room was always part of a working monas-tery, and painted books conceal a vast collection of religious manuscripts.

A RICH GREEN AND GOLD OCTAGONAL LIBRARY

In 1710 when William Benson built Wilbury Park, an Inigo Jones-style hunting lodge in Wiltshire, it was the first Palladian-revival house in England, but by the time Fulke Greville added the octagonal library in 1740 the Georgian taste was well established. Today it retains its original character, with only a bust of Tolstoy to betray the Russian origins of the present owner. A large bay window highlights the gold picked out against the original dark green paintwork. The drawers of the drum-table are marked alphabetically, an early and elegant attempt at a filing system. It is an ideal setting for Lady St Just, literary executor of the American playwright Tennessee Williams, to edit the collection of her old friend's letters to her.

IMPERIAL GRANDEUR AND IRISH GAIETY

Regal bookshelves tower above the library doorway at Clandeboye. Terracotta busts of Greek deities look down, their names inscribed on the panelling below. The family crest surmounting the door announces the colonial ruler who built it, but the room shows that he had a playful side too. A door has been covered with the spines of books so that, when closed, it becomes part of the bookcase; their titles include the names of his children – *Archie's Reflections, Terence's Observations* and *Nellie's Anticipations*. Another bears the title *Open Sesame* to give the game away. The library was the main meeting-place of the house, comfortable with its plum-red carpet and the Persian saddlebag and Gothic needle-work on the chairs.

THE BEST OF RESTORATION AND RECONSTRUCTION

Penrhyn Castle, built in the Norman style in 1820, stands gigantically towered and turreted on a crag overlooking the Menai Strait. Guided by scraps of fabrics, chips of paint and old lithographs, the National Trust has restored three rooms to their original decorations. The drawing room walls and magnificently over-long curtains are of silk and cotton woven in crimson and gold, the oak woodwork is a glowing brown, and two thousand gold stars have been dotted over the vaulted ceiling.

LIGHT-HEARTED DECORATION FROM SACRED SOURCES

Gothick with a 'k' denotes an eighteenth-century interpretation of the medieval architectural style, one that takes outrageous liberties with the shapes and details it pilfers from ecclesiastical sources. Arbury Hall in Warwickshire stands supreme as an example of the genre.

The original Elizabethan house was Gothicized in the mid-eighteenth century for Sir Roger Newdigate, MP for Oxford. Filigreed niches, which should contain pious statues of agonized saints or basins of holy water, have been filled, without the slightest sense of incongruity, with classical nudes and Chinese vases collected by Sir Roger on his Grand Tour. Pulpits have been gaily plundered as the inspiration for plasterwork ceilings. The fireplace in the drawing room is based on a tomb in Westminster Abbey. The dining room even has an aisle, known as 'The Cloister', running beside the arched windows, *top right*. The whole house is a wondrous wedding-cake of a place, expertly iced to vaulted perfection with plaster pinnacles, flowers, tracery and fretwork, which fortunately look far too good to eat.

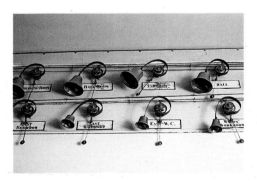

THE STRICT HIERARCHY OF ROOMS BELOW STAIRS

It took armies of servants to keep the grand ancestral homes running smoothly. The numerous domestic tasks, and particularly the preparation of food, required all sorts of equipment and special rooms not found in more modest homes. Although these rooms were never intended to be put on show, they have a pared-down beauty all their own.

Hierarchy amongst the servants of a big house was strictly observed. The butler, cook and housekeeper, in recognition of their status, might be allocated a cross between an office and a sitting room as their private preserve. At Beau Parc in Ireland, *top left*, the housekeeper kept the best china under lock and key in the vaulted still-room, where she did her accounts, hired and fired and, in off-duty hours, could

invite guests. The pine cupboards are painted to resemble rosewood.

Documents, deeds, inventories and other papers relating to family affairs were kept in this high muniment room in a French château, *centre left*. It is now an extremely valuable archive for historians.

The numbered and labelled bells below stairs at Manderston in Scotland, must have been heartily detested by the servants whose duty it was, night and day, to answer their ring. The dairy at Manderston was grandly constructed in marble from seven countries, just to keep the milk cool.

Within the vast Victorian kitchen complex at Lanhydrock House in Cornwall, every culinary operation had its own room. This cast-iron range was the chef's department where he cooked with copper pans; iron pots for plainer cooking were used by lesser mortals in an adjoining scullery.

ICE-COLD STORAGE BEFORE REFRIGERATION

The simple white tiled and marble dairy at Lanhydrock House is the last word in Victorian ingenuity. Ice-cold spring water was piped into channels in the central marble slab and the slate shelf which runs round the room; milk, puddings or bowls of soup were placed on top of these to be kept cool. All the surfaces could be easily and hygienically sluiced down with water. Cream and butter were made next door in one of a succession of separate sculleries.

AN AIR-CONDITIONED AND DECORATIVE LARDER

The estate around Fota, a Regency house on an island in County Cork, was 27,000 acres in its nineteenth-century heyday. The land played a vital part in daily life, both as a playground for its blood-sporting owners and in supplying produce to feed the large household. Game birds, haunches of venison, rabbits, hares, and meat from domestic animals reared and slaughtered on the estate were suspended from this decorative swivelling rack, now hung only with dried

sea lavender and grasses, at the centre of the highly practical octagonal game larder.

The birds – always unplucked – and sides of meat would have been hung for a considerable length of time before they became tender enough for the table. There is fine fly-proof mesh rather than glass across the windows to keep the air fresh. Outside the larder, banks of yew trees were planted to provide shade in summer. The wooden bins round the sides of the stone-flagged room were filled with flour, dried fruits and pulses, and fish were laid flat on the marble slab tops.

CANOPIED ROYAL BEDS AT HATFIELD HOUSE

Queen Elizabeth II was the first guest to sleep in the restored red baroque bed at Hatfield House in Hertfordshire. Sixty-five volunteers spent two years on the painstaking reconstruction based on fragments of old silks and braids found beneath a later Victorian covering. They worked from a full description of the bed and its hangings contained in the original bill for £73, dated 1711 – a miraculous and most timely discovery in Hatfield's archives.

In the next room, *above*, the fresh yellow and blue silk *lit à la Polonaise* is hung against a dark background of Jacobean tapestries.

SLEEPING WITH DREAMS OF HUMAN FOLLIES

Overleaf Every bedroom at the Château de Courances, near the forest of Fontainebleau, has a completely different decorative theme. In this one, the walls and doors are painted wooden panelling, with scenes from La Fontaine's *Fables*, depicting animals and birds acting out man's most imbecilic deeds. Each panel is framed by a band of duck-egg blue. The high-sided sofa bed, placed at the centre of one wall, forms its own enclosed sleeping booth. With an embroidered satin cover and upholstered ends, it also creates a comfortable, and private, sitting room atmosphere during the day.

SPLENDID PAINT TRICKERY TO DECEIVE THE EYE

Inside the Villa Cicogna-Mozzoni, which looks over Lake Lugano in Italy, much is illusory. Architectural features were tricked out of the bare, flat walls by Milanese fresco artists in the sixteenth century. They painted architraves and balustrades, columns, cornices and corners, and false windows and doors. Below the *faux* chair rails they imitated marble and stone; above, they divided the space into panels, painting garlands of fruit, flowers and vegetables or borders of braid, though some panels are now stripped of the paintings that hung there. They topped it all with friezes of crests, cherubs and deer, and coffered ceilings decorated with medallions.

The women had their quarters at the front of the house, and, in this ladies' bedroom, *above and right*, the rush-seated sofa and chairs have soft yellow Spanish leather cushions painted by local artisans to resemble silk brocade. The bed, with its barley-sugar twisted posts, is late seventeenth century, as are the marbled books – village records of Cuasso al Monte drawn up in great detail for Angela Mozzoni, a former chatelaine of the house.

POMPEIAN INSPIRATION FOR A VANISHED ARISTOCRACY

Overleaf The Castle of Lańcut (pronounced 'winezoot') is one of Poland's few surviving reminders of an aristocratic age. The last owner, Count Alfred Potocki, fled the country in 1944 taking six hundred cases of treasures, but it was a mere fraction of what remains. The most sumptuous parts, including this Pompeian room with its rich yellow walls, are eighteenth century. The Etruscan-style friezes and paintings by Vincenzo Brenna were taken from the first engravings made of Pompeii.

MANTELPIECE AND DOORS TRANSFORMED WITH PAINT

Itinerant artists in the seventeenth century painted this fireplace, *left*, and most of the walls, shutters and panelling in the Château de St Marcel-de-Félines.

Drapery in the mistress' study at the Villa Cicogna-Mozzoni, *top left*, is glimpsed through doors encased in marble and stone, with a carved frieze; all of it is achieved with paint. The Chinese room at Burton Constable, *top right*, boasts a lacquered door with carved silver handles and gilded split bamboo finishing the door-surround and chair rail. Panelled double doors at St Marcel-de-Félines, *below left*, have grotesque faces at the centre of each cartouche. Striped banners, spears, helmets and shields surmount a door in the Villa Parisi near Rome, *below right*. The recess of the door is painted to resemble marble.

GRAND ARCHITECTURAL FLOURISHES OF FANCY

Architects and their patrons were quick to see the potential when advances in building techniques allowed a staircase to become an architectural flourish of the grandest possible proportions.

At Luttrellstown in Ireland, *top left*, the walls in the stairwell are *faux marbre*. A portrait of Charles II, above the fireplace, is accompanied by a gallery of his mistresses. Glorious wood-carving of swirling acan-

thus at Sudbury Hall in Derbyshire, *top right*, has been painted in two tones of white. Cantilevered stairs at Burton Constable, *below left*, fill in what had been an open courtyard. The tulip lights on the banisters are a rare survival from days of candlelight. The Grand Stairway of white marble at Kingston Lacy, *below right*, is adorned with fine stone-carvings by Italian craftsmen. *Right* One of an identical pair of staircases at the Palazzo Gangi in Sicily has red marble pilasters and an elaborately worked wrought-iron balustrade.

VICTORIAN PASSIONS PRESERVED UNDER GLASS

Overleaf Nothing has been changed in the first floor saloon at Calke Abbey in Derbyshire since 1841 when the ceiling was raised to accommodate the ancestral portraits. Loose red cotton-damask covers preserve the Victorian chairs beneath in pristine condition. The glass cases lining the walls tell tales of earlier family passions; stuffed birds, seashells and minerals mingle with Egyptian relics.

SIMPLE

The empty room is the starting point for a simple interior,
it sets the style, and even after decoration its lines are still clearly
evident, uncluttered by a multiplicity of colours, objects, or
detailing. Simplicity does not imply lack of sophistication – skilful
choices must be made if it is to be successful. Simple style
rejects the fake, the reproduction and the synthetic, and revels in
the patina of age in original paintwork, the grain of real wood
and the texture of cotton and linen. Its sources can be found in
traditional Scandinavian homes and peasant cottages. It can
be very inexpensive to achieve, or, as Shaker chairs, dhurries and
antique quilts rise in value, deceptively costly.

An unadorned but quietly elegant table is spread with
sparkling old glass. A narrow candle sconce, made doubly bright with a strip
of mirror, hangs above it on the stone-coloured wall. Neutral colours, typical of
Swedish interiors, show up the simple beauty of the objects. The only pure
white element is the little dish and saucer on the table.

There is not one particular style of decoration, as such, which could happily adopt the label 'Simple', yet it perfectly describes an overall approach to interior design. For me, it means interiors where light and space, texture and colour, form and line, are prominent; where each of the elements which go to make up a room has a definite relevance. It is characterized by a positive delight in strong lines; and by a preference for things puritanical, rustic, natural and functional over the artificial and contrived, and for starting the design process with the empty room and allowing that to dictate how it will be decorated and what it will contain rather than imposing a set 'scheme' to a space.

This does not mean that the style need be severe or uncomfortable, bland or boring. What it does mean is that you cannot get away with introducing an object at a whim since it is there to be seen and must relate to everything else in the room. The simple approach is the one I take and the thing I like about it most is that it is open to everyone because it can be based upon ordinary things rather than the costly and rare.

This approach is not an excuse for doing less in terms of decoration and design, nor an easy way out. It stems from an appreciation of the architecture of the building, the proportions of the rooms, the light they receive and the uses to which they are put. Space and light are the greatest luxuries a home can possess and they far outweigh any material luxuries you might introduce. When you pare things down to their simplest, every object, every detail, every colour, pattern and texture is given greater emphasis and must belong or be removed. What you achieve is a strength, a tension between a room and its contents.

In many ways, it takes more confidence to create a simple room than a richly decorative one: confidence in the room itself because that space, those proportions, will be enhanced not hidden; confidence in one's own taste because the things chosen will be thrown into sharp relief with no fudged edges. An attractive window left undressed or adorned with nothing more than a drift of white muslin displays its owner's delight in the basic beauty of the window itself. Drape a window in yards of rich cloth, detailed with pelmets and ties, tassels and lace, and you run the risk of losing it behind art. So often, the use of decorative devices betrays a lack of both confidence and skill. Those who can put pattern against pattern successfully, intricately devising a strong and vibrantly decorative home, are brilliant but few and far between. Taking the simple approach allows far greater scope for success, for self-expression and for creating an environment which will continue to work and give pleasure.

In the way a comfortable, basic chair is difficult to design, so a room made to stand up to years of living, rather than as a show piece requires much care, precision and control. There are no rules except those which you impose but having set your limits and created a framework, then the whole and each part must conform. This may sound austere and regimented, but for advocates of simplicity there must be discipline in design for it to work successfully. Restrictions and limitations can be the key to greater creativity in interior design since they can inspire experiment and exploration in the effort to overcome them.

What the photographs in this chapter show is the stark beauty of a tradition which evolved in Northern Europe and is a combination of peasant rusticity and Protestant understatement. King Gustav III of Sweden gave his name to a style which, in late eighteenth-century Scandinavia, provided a prosperous and grandiose expression of this essentially simple approach. Natural textures, plain walls, strong, pure colours and patterns give a muted background against which occasional touches of gilt and decorative detailing, grand furniture and objects, stand out.

There is an interchange throughout this chapter between the rich and the poor, the decorative and functional, rather than the chasm that might be expected. The interiors shown indicate that the simple approach can encompass eclectic variations, a mixing of old and new, grand and rustic, since all are possible in an unencumbered setting. The elements merely have to suit the room, and cohabit happily. Gustavian style (pages 202-205) uses the plainest wooden floors, the sturdiest forms of ornate furniture, cotton ginghams and checks rather than rich brocades. At the same time, it embraces grand scale, intricate mouldings and detailing and the work of the finest artists in paintings and murals. Yet every detail is easily seen and appreciated.

In the confines of a tiny Breton cottage (pages 190-193), there is fine linen and lace, and sparkling treasures are prominently displayed, yet the framework is simply basic. Wooden fittings carry strong but naive decoration and the lines are clearly strengthened by the use of blue and white paint. Monet's yellow dining room (pages 188-189) borrows from that peasant tradition. The artist chose yellow as his base against which blue and white gingham and china, decorative carving on dressers and white fretwork on chairs, take on a graphic strength in the room. The Breton villagers were restricted to the paint colours used on their boats, to materials which were readily available and to styles of building and furniture that were functional and long-lasting, but Monet consciously chose the clarity and grace of a rustic simplicity in order to create his sunny and relaxed dining room.

The discipline and control of an austere room is a heritage which comes from those who had no choice but to use natural materials with strong colour and pattern and who created things for function rather than display. It can be seen below stairs in the superb kitchens and pantries of great country houses, in peasant homes throughout the world and in the precise but utterly pleasurable designs of the Shaker community in North America.

The simple approach is not easy, but it is achievable given a strong sense of design and full awareness of what you truly admire and enjoy. If you are an incurable collector, incapable of throwing anything away, or if your taste is for the voluptuous, for rococo rather than restraint, then you could not be happy living in a simple room. I prefer to select and edit, to see the inherent structure and form of the things I admire and the rooms I live in.

A PAIR OF COMFORTABLE FARMHOUSE KITCHENS

Both these modern kitchens might be from farmhouses of another century. Although everything in them was specially designed, neither has a high-tech, 'fitted' feel; both have terracotta tiled floors, exposed beams and solid teak work surfaces. In a seventeenth-century cruck-beamed Cumbrian house, *left*, the simplified Mughal arch on the cupboards and the pretty plate shelf are the only elaborations in an otherwise plain room, made yet more successful by the use of a single paint colour. *Above* Here too, in what was once a stable wing, a calming green is the only paint colour, although a coat of ship's varnish on the unpainted plaster gives it a warm patina.

AN ARTS AND CRAFTS SETTING FOR A MODERN COOK

Overleaf Anthony Collett's kitchen – more of an informal living room – is on the first floor of his London house. This decorator has taken his theme from the original Arts and Crafts oak dining table and lattice-back chairs designed by Ambrose Heal around 1900. Tongue and groove boarding covers the walls, topped by a narrow plate shelf displaying Greek pottery, and an old iron stand contains his pots and pans. The long kitchen sideboard with green-painted drawers, rescued from a country house, has a stately presence. All of the modern, functional necessities needed by one who loves to cook are concealed under a dark marble worktop on the opposite wall.

TWO KITCHENS WITH A WELCOMING LACK OF POLISH

For nine years designer Warren Chapman has managed without any plumbing in the three-room tower he uses at weekends. He cooks on a range rescued from a Victorian tenement and uses paraffin stoves for added warmth, *above*. Inspired by colour found in the loggias of Greek houses, he has painted his kitchen and living room dark red.

To create the paint effect on the fireplace, *right*, two young children were given the job of smudging it blue. The marbled wallpaper, pasted on to somewhat haphazardly plastered walls, has been given a coat of varnish to tone it down and protect it.

CLAUDE MONET'S DAFFODIL YELLOW DINING ROOM

Overleaf Claude Monet's three passions in life were his painting, his garden and eating well with his friends. As his eyesight failed in old age, he surrounded himself with brighter tones and more concentrated colour schemes, both in the garden and indoors, to compensate for his increasingly blurred vision. He decorated the otherwise traditionally provincial dining room of his house at Giverny in two vibrating shades of yellow and hung it with Japanese prints and blue and white porcelain – a use of intense colour that was startlingly original in the late nineteenth century.

1

2

3

4

THE STONE HOUSES OF A RUGGED BRETON ISLAND

Life on the windswept island of Ushant, off the Brittany coast, was, until the last generation, both bleak and fanciful. The coastline is too dangerous to fish, so while the women kept sheep and pigs, their menfolk sailed the seas as merchant sailors,

returning with all kinds of treasures and mementoes. There is a childlike love of finery about the ornaments that crowd the thin mantelpieces and plate-racks in the little stone cottages that belies the hardships of life both afloat and ashore. As there are no trees on the island, the houses are furnished from driftwood: it's said that the islanders would pray for 'a fine wreck' from

which to refurbish their homes.

The panelling in the narrow, cruciform passages echoes the bright colours of painted boats. Everything is fitted together with cabin-like ingenuity. The Breton box beds (3 *and* 5), which occupy two-thirds of the ground floor, protect against the cold. Curtains can be drawn for extra warmth. The fireplaces (4 *and* 6) have cupboard

5

6

7

8

doors which are closed to keep out draughts during the night when the fire, fuelled with mud, roots and seaweed, dies down. A rack above the window (8) keeps bread safe from rats, and wooden hooks (1) are for hanging salted hams, not coats.

The two principal rooms are at either end of the tiny cottage. The *pen braou* (*previous page and* 6) is reserved for such

formal occasions as christenings or laying out the dead. The *pen louz* (8) is for daily life, cooking and eating. The contents of the groaning plate-racks (7) speak of long sea journeys to faraway ports; plates and bowls from England and even China were gleaned by the merchantmen. Porcelain flowers under glass domes accompany figurines above the fireplace (6). But, in spite of the

air of fairground gaiety, many of the decorative objects are filled with a deeply religious, mystic significance. Some were brought to the island by sailors as thanks-offerings for a safe return; others, such as the mirrored glass witch balls that hang from the beams and the mantelpiece (6), commemorate pilgrimages to religious festivals in mainland France.

A TWENTIETH-CENTURY EXTENSION IN MEDIEVAL STYLE

A rugged dining room has been created in a recent addition to the fifteenth-century gatehouse of a castle in Glamorgan. The present opening to the stairs was once the front door, and this new room now connects the gatehouse with the kitchen, formerly the porter's lodge. The walls, plastered with lime mortar, have been lightly decorated by the owner with a simple frieze painted in earth colours. Square-leaded windows, which fit well with the rest of the building, were made in traditional manner by local craftsmen, as was the Welsh earthenware on the floor. The sycamore plates and bowls are in daily use.

DIGNIFIED SIMPLICITY FOR A GENTLEMAN'S DINING ROOM

A taste for the simple, solid and dignified is perfectly demonstrated in this kitchen and dining room in a long, low cottage amid Hertfordshire cornfields. A very dark green, almost black, dado is combined with creamy yellow paintwork, providing an appropriately masculine setting for a generous round oak table, plain wooden chairs and a group of animal pictures. The owner believes large pieces of furniture make a small room appear bigger. A bunch of wild flowers, a collection of crooks, mallets and racquets, and hats casually hung on a pair of tall antlers are the finishing details of this unmistakably English country room.

A GERMAN ARTIST'S
SET PIECE LIVING ROOM

There are six living rooms in the 400-year-old house on the southern edge of the Black Forest owned by the abstract artist, Karl-heinz Scherer. His interiors reflect his paintings, stripped to a stark beauty. He allows no richness or ceremony, and he wishes that the rooms were even emptier. Many of us have a niggling urge to attempt such a degree of self-discipline and it only takes a little extra confidence to attain.

Here, the effect is achieved with three closely related shades of bird's egg green – made by mixing leftover pots of paint and ordinary white – used on the bare floorboards, walls and wooden panelling; it would work equally well with yellows, pinks or greys. The Biedermeier sofa with its black leather cover and matching table and chair have an obvious elegance, but a matched trio of table and chairs in any style could equal their panache.

INEXPENSIVE STYLE IN BLACK AND WHITE

The architecture student who devised this room for herself has restricted her palette severely – even the collection of assorted engravings is unified by their absence of colour and their sedate black frames. The chintz on the seats of the three matching chairs (found for £1 each) has been dyed black, but its original pattern still shows through, giving an effect of expensive damask. The table was so scruffy that she covered it with a generous, pristine white cloth, creating the effect of an altar, and set the ensemble against white walls unblemished by any cornice or mouldings.

The old Turkish rug on the bare floorboards and the wooden chairs soften and relieve the contrasting black and white of this simple space. The owner's resourcefulness and good eye have more than compensated for a lack of money in creating a stylish interior.

COLOUR AND TEXTURE
IN AN ARTIST'S KITCHEN

Artist James Reeve surrounds himself at home with the colours he uses in his paintings so he still feels amongst them when he comes in from the studio. In the extended kitchen and dining room of his thatched Devonshire cottage, he has dabbed raw sienna oil paint over a coat of white emulsion to 'break' the colour in a manner suited to the unevenly plastered walls. The effect is like rich clotted cream or pale tortoiseshell. Antique carpets and a patch-work tablecloth add richness of colour and texture; they are part of a collection of textiles which ranges from old evening gowns to ecclesiastical copes.

The space was created by knocking through two meanly proportioned rooms and supporting the ceiling with a handsome sixteenth-century cross beam from a de-molished building in Exeter. At the dining end of the room the furniture is quite grand, but the dark wood of the oak settle and chairs combines well with the beam and the countrified kitchen area. A keen cook, he keeps the *batterie de cuisine* to hand, hung from the hexagonal wooden post, the top of which is also his chopping block, beside the long, scrubbed pine preparation table.

A BRIGHT, FRESH TREATMENT
FOR A SCOTTISH LODGE

Overleaf It takes twenty years to break in new leather, according to the owner of this comfortable study in a shooting lodge beside Loch Tay. Preferring not to wait for new chairs to age, he has extended the useful life of an old pair of club-like armchairs, their dark leather broken in, by re-covering the crumbling seat cushions with chintz. The print, also used on a small gilt chair, has added country freshness to what would have otherwise been rather sombre furniture. The tongue and groove boarding, painted a sunny yellow, adds another light touch, and the black-framed engravings, well grouped around the fire-place, make the visual link between the yellow paint and the black chairs.

1

2

3

4

5

SWEDISH ELEGANCE OF THE GUSTAVIAN PERIOD

Svindersvik (*previous page and* 6), is one of the oldest surviving summer houses on the outskirts of Stockholm. It was built in the mid-eighteenth century for Claes Grill, an East Indian merchant of Italian extraction, and then refurbished during the reign of Gustav III (1771–92) in what is known as the Gustavian style. Gustav was an active patron of the arts, he founded the Swedish Academy, and greatly admired the contemporary French style of Louis XVI.

Svindersvik and these other interiors from houses in and around Stockholm, epitomize the Gustavian style: its

6

7

8

9

10

11

strong French influence is tempered by a home-grown tendency to simplify grandeur. Walls are painted rather than panelled, and in many rooms mouldings are indicated by painted lines. The furniture, despite its curved lines, is seldom gilded, but lacquered or painted in matt greys, and upholstered in such humble cottons as gingham. Bleached floors are left bare rather than carpeted with Savonnerie but the mere presence of the ubiquitous stoves (2, 4 and 7), with their decorative tiled casings, banishes any thought of chilliness. It is a classic style, humble and grand, suited to elegant little country cottages and island retreats, as well as summer palaces such as Svindersvik.

CLIFFSIDE ROOMS CARVED IN STONE

A house created out of a series of caves hewn from the living rock would surely win any simple-life competition. That is exactly what these two rooms are – part of a troglodyte settlement, honeycombed inside a cliff in the Loire district of France. The caves owe their existence in part to the many nearby châteaux which were often built out of blocks of creamy tufa quarried from these local cliffs. The warren of caves that resulted became storage spaces for wine, hiding-places for resistance workers and were finally joined together by long tunnels and staircases, and domesticated.

The sitting room fireplace, *left*, is carved straight out of the rock in a classical French countrified shape, with pilasters flat against the wall above the chimneypiece. The ceiling is timbered and beamed as a safeguard against falls of rock and is painted with a design of birds and water lilies. The bathroom fireplace, *above*, has been constructed from blocks of stone set against the wall. The ceiling is glossy white tongue and groove planking. There are shiny beeswaxed bricks laid on the floor and very simple white-painted furniture.

Light streams into these cave rooms from the outside world through perfectly normal windows and doors, which, while performing their function, do look a little strange to a casual passer-by who sees them perching unexpectedly, half-way up a cliff face.

SPLENDID BARENESS IN A RENAISSANCE HOUSE

The dress designer who owned this six-teenth-century house in Antwerp had a taste for bare luxury. In her bedroom, white walls, careless white linen curtains, dark-

beamed ceiling and polished floorboards are the backdrop for the select few pieces of furniture. The spareness, epitomized by the Empire iron campaign chair, left deliber-ately without any upholstery, is enriched by a collection of silver on a simple table topped with black marble.

PRISTINE BEDS IN NOSTALGIC SURROUNDINGS

These two rooms, *right*, have a simplicity that recalls servants' bedrooms of a century or more ago. With their pairs of decorative cast-iron or polished metal bedsteads,

208

pristine cotton covers, whitewashed walls and plain floors, they are as neat as a new pin. Devoid of pictures or other frippery these rooms are crisply welcoming for a weekend guest, though one room, *top*, is so compact that the only place available to stow any belongings is underneath the bed.

A BEDROOM REDUCED TO MEDITERRANEAN ESSENTIALS

Overleaf Uneven surfaces and a blue and white colour scheme suggest a Greek island *pension*, but this bedroom is in fact in an eighteenth-century brick tower in England.

The owner sculpted all the mouldings, the fireplace, bed base and picture frames out of cement, then softened the contours by pasting over sheets of newspaper before painting everything the mattest of whites. A printer's typecase has been used to display a collection of butterflies.

NATURAL COLOURS FOR A SIMPLE BATHROOM

It is not easy to make a bathroom as simple as this, without it feeling cold and spartan. But the walls have been painted a warm shade of pale straw, complementing the natural coir flooring. Cosy tongue and groove boarding hides the plumbing and provides a shelf for objects that are both functional and decorative. A cushioned window-seat adds a comfortable touch.

A CENTRED BATH BENEATH EXPOSED BEAMS

Overleaf The bath stands proudly in the centre of this room – an ideal solution when the ceiling slopes very steeply. Green-grey walls and putty-coloured woodwork, rush matting and the patina of a French provincial cupboard, combine to soothe and relax. The simple luxury of painted Regency chairs, tables and towel-rail provides continuity with the adjoining bedroom.

AN EXACTING FRENCH EYE FOR DETAIL

When the owner of this bathroom in a minute Parisian apartment in the Faubourg St Germain lies in her bed, this is what she sees – the bedroom and bathroom are combined. An Indian cotton sari, one of several which she alternates, is very simply draped, but it effectively hides the bath from view. A soft white skirt, generously pleated and tucked, disguises the washbasin and any clutter.

The eye for detail is exacting: a low ceiling has been lifted visually by painting the heavy beams white, an oval mirror recalls the shape of the porthole window, and the red towels hanging beside the washbasin intensify the blue freshness of the room. Identical vases, one in white, one in black, echo the contrasts in the blue and white striped chintz used on walls and for curtains. A gentle Indian-inspired cotton, also patterned in blue and white, covers the comfortable armchair. The same fabric covers the bed on the opposite side of the room.

SHABBY CHIC

Rejection of the new and shiny in favour of the battered
and antique is an approach found all over the world, but which is
most fundamentally English. Sometimes it is the result of
making the best of circumstances when there is no money to
repair, restore, reconstruct or replace; in other cases it is quite
deliberate, a celebration of time having passed. It is not an easy
style to achieve, in the wrong hands the effect can be as
depressing and impoverished as a run-down boarding house,
but put together by an expert the worn leather chairs, faded
fabrics, mended china, mellow peeling paint and scuffed furniture
contribute to an atmosphere that is welcoming and rich.

The tranquil beauty of Lady Astley, drawn in Rome
by Joseph Severn in 1848, hangs serenely at the centre of an honestly contrived and
deliberately shabby still life in the drawing room at Crowsley Park. The nail holes pitting
the eighteenth-century panelling have been left defiantly unfilled.

By a strange coincidence, the day I was invited to write this introduction I saw a movie, *Withnail and I*, a large part of which was set in a cottage in the Welsh countryside. The interior of the cottage, with its good but neglected pieces of furniture, crumbling and stained plaster walls haphazardly hung with ravishing and unselfconscious pictures and looking glasses, faded and tattered curtains and other fabrics, was for me an embodiment of the term Shabby Chic.

'Chic' is simply style, used with an élan that has a social or intellectual overtone. A basement flat furnished with an old cretonne-covered sofa can be shabby chic if it has this ingredient, as can a Bauhaus flat in Berlin, or a room in a grand ancestral house, or a room specially put together by the High Priest of the genre, London dealer, Christopher Gibbs.

I think that rooms that have been visibly 'decorated' fall into two categories, one of comfort, and the other of ostentation or showiness. Shabbiness will always be of the former, with the chic appearing as effortless understatement.

Shabbiness, apart from its obvious aesthetic appeal, is the only defence and bastion against ostentation and mis-spent money. For furniture and cloth to have arrived at a shabby state usually implies that the things were of good quality and built to last back in their hey-day. So it does not matter a fig if they are scuffed, worn, out of date, or out of fashion – so much the better in fact. It is the traces of the haphazards of living that bring things to life and give them reality, and reality is what shabby chic is all about.

When a house has survived the occupation of several generations of one family, unless they were all very plain personalities, a definite but fragile atmosphere is left behind and benign ghosts begin to inhabit. If they are there, and they are extremely precious if they are, they can be pleaded with not to depart but can only be preserved by a careful and gentle approach to the restorations that may have to be done to stop the house falling apart.

I shall never forget seeing the library at Chastleton House in Warwickshire, before it was restored in the 1960s. It had a very powerful atmosphere, and you could so easily have imagined that perhaps Cromwell's men had stormed through three hundred years before and that it had not been touched since. Shelves sagged with the weight of books, some still upright and others all fallen on to their sides; large volumes higgledy-piggledy on a table in the centre of the small room; dust everywhere. The shelves were, I think, unpainted and of raw oak, the walls a crumbling brown – it was delicious. But alas, when I returned a few years later, the shelves had been straightened and painted white, the walls were red and the ghosts had departed. Genuine remnants of the past are so fragile, and so precious, that you hardly dare to breathe when you are given the immensely responsible job of trying to preserve and restore them.

To be able to reproduce a look of authentic shabbiness requires an exhaustive knowledge of the past and an eye that is trained to be aware of the slightest nuance of colour and texture, joined with an imagination that is capable of making one of those intuitive leaps in the dark and getting it right. To be able to reproduce convincingly that look which is the result of years of use and fair wear and tear is the greatest of all decorating talents.

Colour, which is so very important and critical has been sadly misused over the past thirty years. Our eyes, alas, have been blunted by a colour spectrum that is too bright and too strong. Colour photography often comes to us in ghastly saturated hues, the inevitable result I suppose of advancing technology. Nine out of ten colour television sets are maladjusted; and hideously chromatic chemical dyes are used as the base tints for mixing colourized decorating paints. Sometime ago an architect showed me a colour chart which had been issued by a manufacturer of distemper before the last war. Distemper was the paint used on interior walls before the advent of emulsions. Everything on that chart by today's standards might be considered dirty and dingy – but oh! what subtlety, every shade a possible. Lovely soft grey-greens, ochres and reds, each with a dozen different pigments in them. What a huge amount of colour sensitivity we have lost, along with so much else during the last decades. If we had not lost this sensitivity there would be a tremendous uproar over some of the cleaned, scrubbed would be a better word, paintings hanging in our national collections today where in some many cases the real 'signature' of the artist has been lost for ever, leaving behind simply the underpainting. What joy it was to see Titian's *The Entombment of Christ* from the Prado hung uncleaned in the 'Genius of Venice' exhibition at the Royal Academy a few years ago.

If, when you are trying to restore, you don't have the advantage of hand-me-downs from past generations, keep an eye for even and subtle colour tonality. Jump about, with your dogs, on expensive new materials before making the loose covers; or better still don't be afraid to use inexpensive printed fabrics that come in rather sharp colours, because the design and background can be made to tone together and the whole thing become perfectly acceptable after a dip in cold tea or coffee, or even (as I have done) soaked in a solution of liquid seaweed fertiliser. Remember words like 'fair wear and tear', '*maigre*', and 'kicked about a bit'; and most important, keep asking yourself as you place furniture and ornaments 'does it look as though it has always been there?' Beware of the Biedermeier style if it is over decorated: the true humble folk's furniture was very simple, produced for people who did not have a lot of money. Nothing that is still serviceable should be thrown away or discarded just because it has been superseded by something more fashionable.

Remember that the way Edwardian ladies really wore their dresses was a far cry from the perfectly groomed and turned out women that Cecil Beaton confronted us with for the Ascot scenes in the film *My Fair Lady*. To have appeared anywhere with that amount of finish would at the time have been considered as 'actressy' or worse. The society journals from the early years of the century show exactly what I mean. I think that the aim should be for a room where, no matter what you do in it, you can feel confident that none of the ornaments will fall off their perches in horror.

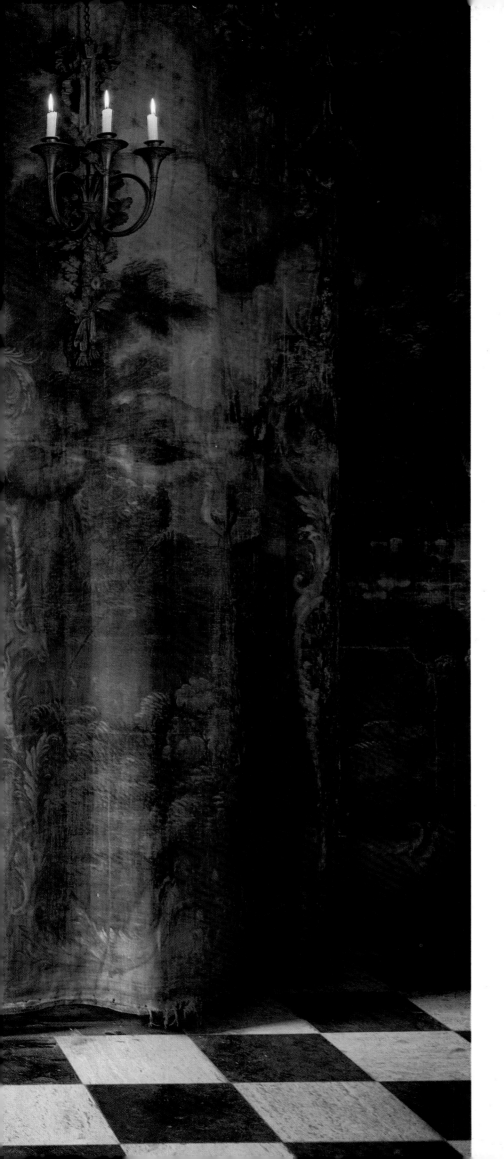

PAINTED CANVAS LEFT WELL ALONE TO AGE

A small doorway in the hall at Southside House, near Wimbledon Common, leads into what was once the powder closet where eighteenth-century ladies and gentlemen had their wigs freshly whitened with powder. The brass handle and lock shine, though the wood is scuffed and scratched. The walls are covered with the original late seventeenth-century painted canvas – sometimes a substitute for more costly tapestry or tooled leather – which now billows out from the wall, its colours subdued by years of dust. Candles still burn in the sconces. Only the fresh red lining and hem of the curtain, giving it a few more years of service, show any evidence of modern interference. This is genuine faded grandeur, where the occupants of the house have left a richly decorated interior simply to age in its own way.

WINDOWS DRESSED WITH ANTIQUE FABRICS

Nothing is more evocative than faded old fabrics. Here, windows and doors from a nineteenth-century French convent have been adorned with antique stuffs, *above*. Only the ragged early-Victorian silk curtains, *below left*, are a matching pair. The rich assortment of nineteenth-century Paisley shawls, made more dramatic by a green blind, *top right*, and the 1890s sprigged saris, trimmed with slightly older tasselled braid, *top left*, were never originally intended to be used as curtains. Teamed with modern

reproductions of antique wallpapers, their genuine age is half their charm. The confection of appliquéd muslin and trimmed and embroidered cream lace, *below right*, recalls Miss Havisham's wedding dress in Charles Dickens' *Great Expectations*.

Fine Regency rose damask curtains, *right*, faded by the sun and generously looped over magnificent gilded rosettes, hang in the drawing room windows of a grand old Irish house, looking down a grassy bank to the River Boyne below. The contrasting fine net curtains, barely touching a pair of gilt ballroom chairs, are merely nylon, hung over lace-trimmed Holland blinds.

AN HISTORIC HALL
FURNISHED WITH JUNK

A massive mahogany sideboard, of a date much later than the eighteenth-century house, was bought for £5 to fill up a huge entrance hall at Crowsley Park. Hand-marbled walls have been left untouched since they were painted in the mid-nineteenth century and the present inhabitants have not meddled, save to cover the worst patches of damage with prints. Kitchen jars are used as vases and there is no attempt to disguise the humble bentwood chairs. The worn walls and cracked cornice are left to establish the character of the place.

CARELESS CONFIDENCE
AND A SENSE OF THEATRE

The interior decorator who owns this tiny Paris apartment has an innate sense of theatre. The atmosphere is part nursery, part bazaar, part stage: a place where dozens of precariously balanced, sweet-coloured objects offer themselves to the sticky fingers of her young children. She does not care that things are chipped, scuffed, worn or even incomplete. Swathes of fabric are draped over chairs, tasselled braid is pinned around table rims, nothing matches, and you feel that any moment the scenery may change before your eyes.

A ROOM FADED BUT NOT DULLED BY TIME

In the years after Nelson's death, Lady Hamilton played endless games of patience in the drawing room of Southside House. Now, the echoes of its former grandeur can barely be heard. All the elements of this once richly gold room, furnished with the fruits of an eighteenth-century Grand Tour, have taken on complementary hues and tones. Few changes or additions have been made to destroy its continuity, though, inevitably, items have disappeared, the upholstery velvet has faded and the painted furniture dulled. But the room still has a glamour of its own.

A CONSCIOUS REJECTION OF CULTIVATED STYLE

A lovely Edwardian portrait of a young girl hangs in the drawing room at Crowsley Park, one of an assortment of pictures tightly packed to hide the patches of bare brick and plaster. The inhabitants care little about finish or disrepair, but the apparent muddle on the sideboard is not entirely accidental. The leather-bound volumes, the oil lamp without a shade, the woven baskets and the dried flowers and seed heads, add to the carefree dilapidation. This cultivation of decay is deliberately irreverent, yet the portrait shows that their tastes are far from careless.

ENDLESSLY LAUNDERED EDWARDIAN CHINTZ

Overleaf The panelled parlour created for the wife of an industrialist in his Scottish shooting lodge was decorated in a style confidently brand spanking new, with gleaming white plasterwork and light airy carpets and upholstery, all part of the Edwardian rejection of dark mid-Victorian rooms. Now the servants who brushed, dusted and endlessly laundered the loose chintz covers are gone, and the place is settling into dignified old age. Its creator would probably deplore its shabbiness, but the room has been so beautifully cared for that its delicate charm is as strong as ever.

CRUMBLING LEATHER AND PILES OF BOOKS

The first floor library at Southside House is already so crowded with pieces of furniture, pictures and books that it would be difficult to add anything new, and nothing worn or faded has been replaced either, so the room retains its comfortable tranquillity. The curtains have long since disappeared and no attempt has been made to disguise the necessary modern wiring beside the door. The floorboards are only sparsely covered with rugs. But the well-worn leather sofa with its big, battered cushions, the leather reclining-chair, the overflowing bookcases and the mint-green walls, marked with the imprint of generations of changing tastes in pictures, speak of years of familiarity and ease. It is an atmosphere that, once lost, can never be artificially recreated.

VISUAL ANARCHY IN AN OXFORDSHIRE MANSION

A strange mixture of attic and jumble-sale furnishings has crept inside the shell of an ornate and grandly-conceived mansion. Crowsley Park in Oxfordshire, almost a ruin after years of neglect, was let rent-free to two architects on condition that it was not allowed to deteriorate further. They have gradually mended the house and made it habitable, but have not altered anything just for the sake of appearance. Layers of past decoration have been uncovered – the eighteenth-century panelling in the drawing room was found beneath later panelling, wallpaper and canvas – but not restored. Objects are welcomed as long as they are useful or beautiful or loved. Even the 1960s paper lampshade is acceptable since it adequately fulfils its function.

ECHOES OF ANGLO-IRISH SPLENDOUR

The drawing room of Beau Parc in County Meath was last decorated in the final flush of Anglo-Irish viceregal confidence and power. It has scarcely been changed since those Edwardian days. A low, amply padded sofa, smothered in immensely fat cushions, still wears its well-creased pale pink damask cover. Pictures of the house and nearby River Boyne, painted in the eighteenth century by Thomas Roberts, hang, dark and uncleaned, on the cracking green paint-work. Collections of china still fill the glass-fronted boulle cabinets inlaid with ormolu and decorated with tortoiseshell.

INVITING CUSHIONS AND ROSE-PATTERNED COVERS

Nothing but the best was the motto followed by Mrs Whitaker when she redecorated Pylewell Park at the turn of the century. Looking at the house today, largely untouched, the luxury of the period is still evident. She furnished the Pink Bedroom with downy silk-covered cushions, comfortable chairs, a seamless carpet, woven especially for the room in 1905, a generously proportioned mirror, and a garland-painted eighteenth-century four-poster bed. The pleated bed hangings and the covers for the sofa and chairs are the same glazed rose-patterned chintz she originally chose.

THREE STYLES OF OLD-FASHIONED COMFORT

The quality of the simple furniture and fabric in this guest room in the Château de Montgeoffroy, *left*, though faded, is still apparent. The same flower-patterned material is used for wall and bed hangings, curtains, and covers. Its muted colours complement the patina of the original eighteenth-century panelling and floor.

Matching Italianate beds in Sandbeck House in Yorkshire, *above*, with tattered, once-sage-green damask and bedposts covered in honey-coloured velvet, still have a beauty of their own which is set off by pristine white bedcovers of lace and linen.

A footstool is needed to reach this high bed in the Château de Courances. An aromatic branch has been tied to the old-fashioned silk lampshade overhanging it. Bed and walls are covered with the same floral print, but the eye is distracted by a wonderful collection of pictures.

ECCENTRIC

Some houses can never really be categorized.
The people who create them follow no fashions, adhere to no
rules and are above criticism – their houses are a genuine key
to their characters. The owners exhibit an unbounded,
self-indulgent confidence in their own taste, caring not for
the opinion of others. The interiors range from theatrical excesses
in silks, satins and furs, to a house turned into a suite of
playrooms filled with toys and dolls by a middle-aged couple,
tired of being governed by adult conventions. The rooms all have
true originality and in their apparent madness and anarchy less
brave souls can find inspiration to follow and adapt.

The most striking element in an architect's sitting room in Provence
is a rack, originally intended for drying bottles. It now conceals a burglar alarm
while playing host to an assortment of objects: silvered flowers and bottles, a cheese
grater and a benign household god – the Polynesian straw mask.

Interiors are supposed to reveal everything about the people who make and inhabit them, even if in some cases the clues are pretty well hidden. But in an eccentric house there is no need to study the titles on the bookshelves or scrutinize the bathroom accessories to see exactly what is going on. You are immediately transported to a world where individual vision has triumphed over all the rules, conventions and ordinary usages. Eccentric decoration is not a style or even a family of styles united by a common theme: it is a state of mind. You cannot deliberately set out to create an eccentric interior and be convincing. Conceivably, someone might adapt an odd idea, like the four-poster bathtub on pages 248-249, and have some success with it, but that is not the point. These decorators are individualists to whom originality comes as naturally as breathing.

Thorough-going eccentrics are oblivious of public opinion, blithely unconcerned about the vagaries of taste and undefeated by everyday obstacles such as lack of time and money. It took 'Picassiette', Raymon Edouard Isidore, thirty years of 'scrounging' to encrust his home and *all* his possessions with a mosaic of broken china; a miracle of decorative vision, patience and economy (pages 240-241). It is not recorded how Mme Isidore felt about the transformation of her stove and sewing machine into part of her husband's artistic dream.

In conventional decorating terms, it is accepted that slightly off-beat, personal touches inject vitality into what could otherwise be rooms of bland good taste. In eccentric interiors, everything is quirky. There is an abundance of life. Something about mundane objects inspires eccentrics to invest them with meaning and juxtapose them in topsy-turvy arrangements that challenge the natural order of things – like a chandelier made of flowerpots, say – what Edith Sitwell, a true eccentric, describes in her study of *English Eccentrics* as 'a mania for symbolisation'. There is often a chain reaction of associations, at the end of which is laughter. Eccentricity, when it is not deadly serious, is a tremendous joke.

There is also a certain talent for improvisation and a disregard for the accepted virtues of housekeeping. Dust and neglect are not incompatible with eccentric decor, nor is the kind of tearing-rush DIY approach in which the perpetrator feels compelled to translate visions into an immediate reality before the inspiration is lost. But eccentrics can be meticulous, too. If there is sometimes glue instead of curtain headings, askew carpentry and a cheerful coexistence with mice, beetles and spiders, there is also the ability to carry through grand or fixed ideas, beyond the point less persistent people would go. Uncharitably, some people might call this the art of obsession.

Ordinary objects are transformed in the hands of some eccentrics, others get hold of an idea such as decorating everything they possess with mosaic, and carry it to an illogical conclusion. Then there are those who go directly in search of the macabre and bizarre preferring to share their surroundings with skulls, mementoes *mori*, savage stuffed animals and frighteningly realistic reptiles. The intention, perhaps, is to stimulate the directness of feeling – a *frisson* of shock – normally only experienced by children.

There is also the type of decorator whose eccentricity has to do with exaggeration. The difference between these interiors and more traditional rooms is one of quantity rather than quality. Double tie-backs or curtains of extravagant length, pairs of swagged borders, indulgence in luxurious fabrics, gilt and mirrors, frills on frills, bear rugs over sheepskins – the result may look like a parody of conventional taste but this theatricality really betrays a love of decorating for its own sake.

Eccentricity is particularly associated with the British, a prejudice blithely explained away by Edith Sitwell as owing to 'the peculiar and satisfactory knowledge of infallibility that is the hallmark and birthright of the British nation'. There is certainly a long history of folly-building in Britain – weird and wonderful houses in the shapes of pineapples, triangles, pyramids, animal mausoleums, on which eccentric architectural impulses have been focussed. As the following chapter shows, however, eccentricity in decoration is not a British prerogative.

Obviously, eccentrics please themselves. For the rest of us, whether or not we understand the language, these anarchic interiors, fizzing with energy and joy, are an antidote to what is safe and expected.

A PASSION FOR WHAT OTHER PEOPLE THREW AWAY

In the early 1930s, an odd-job man in Chartres, Raymon Edouard Isidore, announced to his wife that he had an idea for decorating their home. Inspired, he said, by a superior force, he set about glorifying the house with murals and mosaics entirely made of broken china, glass and other detritus set in cement – creating beauty from the discarded. By the time of his death in 1964, he had covered every surface with patterns and pictures, including the exterior

facade of the house and a small chapel. Celebrated as a naïve artist, he became known as *Picassiette*, 'The Scrounger'.

The kitchen, *left and above left*, was the first room he decorated; the cooking stove, like all the furniture, is covered with a floral pattern, while the walls and door are painted with daisies. In their bedroom, *top and above right*, a mural of an Arabian scene, with camels, bedouin and palm trees, covers one wall, while a view of Chartres' Pont Neuf covers another. Madame Isidore's encrusted sewing machine stands before the mirrored cupboard.

SILKS AND BOWS IN A HATTER'S SITTING ROOM

David Shilling approaches the decoration of his home in much the same way as he trims the flamboyant hats that he designs. In his sitting room he has conjured up the gilt, silks, lace and mirrors of an exclusive, turn-of-the-century Parisian milliner's showroom in unashamed expression of his personality. None of the elements in this uncluttered room is particularly strange in itself, except perhaps the Victorian goldfish-bowl stand which has been made into a stool, but everything is exaggerated. The length of the curtains of ivory silk and antique embroidered net, spilling over on to the carpet, is intentionally profligate. There are two tiers of tie-backs. Bows are tied everywhere, even on the cake stand.

A GRAVELY HUMOROUS OBSESSION

The owner of this domestic mausoleum in Hampstead is neither sinister nor obsessed with thoughts of death; she is a robustly cheerful student of architecture who is amused by her own taste for the macabre. Her bedroom, with its draped furniture and cornice of black lace hung with bows of satin ribbon, evokes the atmosphere of a Victorian funeral parlour. Charms, cruci-fixes, gilt plaster cherubs and other religious and memorial ephemera, rescued from junk shops and flea markets, have been resur-rected on an ornate marbled cabinet, amid black net and mourning feathers. In other rooms, dead flowers and guttering candles add dramatically to the effect, described by the creator as 'Gothique'.

A VARIETY OF ANIMAL ENTHUSIASMS MADE PUBLIC

The elephants and painted palm fronds, decorating the Moorish arch leading into this bathroom, *left*, set a haphazard African theme, taken up in the African textiles hanging on the walls and the leopard spots painted on the bath. A ram's head conceals the taps, and rust-coloured curtains of waterproof cotton are suspended over the bath from an old wheelchair wheel.

The owner of this collection, *top left*, may not have set out to shock, but one suspects that he is not displeased if a visitor is startled by the stuffed ape, skulls or tribal artefacts displayed in an otherwise conventionally painted room.

Inspired by the film *Cleopatra*, this bedroom, *top right*, has been transformed into a homage to ancient Egypt. The Pharaoh's head was carved from hardening plaster of Paris to look like weathered stone. The various Nile reptiles advancing over the carpet were all bought from junk shops.

In the tropical setting of a *trompe-l'oeil* artist's bedroom, *above left*, most surfaces, including the palm pelmet, have been painted with lush foliage and jungle animals. The arctic presence of a collection of carved Swiss serving bears is not so surprising if you know that the owner once painted the bodywork of a London taxi-cab to look like pink, buttoned silk.

A window-seat, *above right*, embroidered with a writhing snake, has been carefully positioned in a painter's cottage, to emphasize the disturbing collection of reptiles on the deep sill.

INDULGING IN A SECOND CHILDHOOD

Daisy Rogers spent her childhood with a father who did not approve of dolls or model trains, and she spent much of her adult, married life dusting. So when she married for the second time, she and her late husband, Rogey, decided to have their childhood over again. Twenty years ago, they turned the three floors above his North London antique shop into a vast playroom, filled with dolls, model houses and trains, and naughty seaside postcards.

They painted the walls, cupboards, doors and ceilings with their own decorations, mainly in the two colours that came from a

job lot of paint – Kingfisher Blue and Siamese Pink – and Daisy never, ever, did any dusting. Rogey was the carpenter, making model factories, buildings and bleak industrial landscapes round a toy railway which stopped working because of the dust. Many of the buildings are models of real ones, taken from photographs in Daisy's 250 albums. Daisy collected hundreds of dolls – nearly a thousand in one room alone – and made costumes for them, starting with the Dark Ages and continuing through the centuries up to an astronaut in his spacesuit on the final shelf.

Rogey built a four-inch-deep canal bridge on their bedroom mantelpiece, *above*, from which a canalboat, hung with bunting

and called 'Daisy', is emerging. A terrace of Georgian houses and shops co-exists with a Wild West barn and stables, and a pub interior hung with fairy lights.

The kitchen, *left*, is a cheerful mass of colour, compensation for the lack of hot water and heating. The unicorn-head bottles of bubble bath glow against their Alpine background. When the walls crumbled in the kitchen, Daisy covered the cracks with calico sheets dipped in plaster of Paris, which dried in unyielding folds and swags.

The womb-like bathroom, *above*, with Guy Fawkes masks stuck on the wall, was hastily painted to get it looking colourful. On the stairway, *right*, huge flaming eyes seem to wink and glare as you pass.

FOUR-POSTER BATH IN A PROVENCAL BATHROOM

Overleaf Open fireplaces and four-poster baths are rare even in the most lavish bathrooms, but they are features enjoyed by the younger guests who stay in the warren of attic rooms at the top of an old Provençal farmhouse. In the bathroom, a virtue was made out of economic necessity; the bare cemented walls were left in their original state, and the concrete floor simply painted white. Minimal strips of unhemmed fabric in four different patterns of blue and white were taped, glued and nailed around the bath. There is the utmost disregard of finish, but a striking effect.

DECORATIVE WHIMS OF AN ENGLISH AESTHETE

Wilsford Manor was Stephen Tennant's greatest creation. He painted, he wrote, he loved and collected shells and friends, but completed little in the way of a life's work other than his beloved house, which is a brave mixture of precious furniture and theatrical junk. In the dining room, *right*, a late-Victorian copy of a George II

gilt mirror sits shamelessly beside a fine eighteenth-century Italian console table, one of an unmatched six in this room alone. The room is lit by warm tungsten (not fluorescent) strips hidden behind a plaster cornice of pink-painted scallop shells. Double-swagged paper borders appear, in different colours, in every major room. In an opulent bedroom, *above*, polar bear, zebra, leopard and pony skins are scattered over a carpet of lamb's fleeces.

Disregard for convention could have no greater demonstration than Stephen Tennant's curtains on an upper landing, *previous page*: the seventeenth-century style of the house calls for tapestry and velvet, but the windows have been dressed with triple-frilled confections of satin and taffeta. The cornice is papered with gold foil beneath a glossy pink ceiling, and aged straw hats are stored on ornate plant stands and the staircase newel posts.

PHOTOGRAPHIC ACKNOWLEDGMENTS

THE PHOTOGRAPHS IN THIS BOOK WERE TAKEN BY THE FOLLOWING PEOPLE:

2 Lucinda Lambton; 8 François Halard; 10 Richard Bryant; 14-15 Fritz von der Schulenburg; 15 above right Jacques Dirand; 15 below right François Halard; 16 left John Vere Brown; 16-17 Dennis Krukowski; 18-21 John Vere Brown; 22-23 1 Jacques Dirand, 2 James Merrell, 3 Jacques Dirand, 4 Karen Radkai, 5 Arabella McNair Wilson, 6 James Mortimer, 7 Jean Pierre Godeaut, 8 Dennis Krukowski, 9 Clive Frost, 10 Fritz von der Schulenburg, 11 Bill Batten, 12 Lucinda Lambton; 24 John Vere Brown; 25 Tom Leighton; 26-27 Jacques Dirand; 28-29 Bill Batten; 30-32 Lucinda Lambton; 33 Jacques Dirand; 34-35 John Vere Brown; 36 James Mortimer; 37 Tom Leighton; 38-72 James Mortimer; 73 above James Mortimer; 73 below Michael Boys; 74-75 James Mortimer; 76 above left Michael Boys; 76 below left James Mortimer; 76-77 Michael Boys; 78-79 Roland Beaufre; 80-81 James Mortimer; 84-85 James Mortimer; 86-87 Fritz von der Schulenburg; 88 James Mortimer; 89 David Montgomery; 90 left, above and below James Mortimer; 90-91 François Halard; 92-96 James Mortimer; 97 above Chris Drake; 97 below Bill Batten; 98-99 James Mortimer; 100 James Wedge; 101-103 James Mortimer; 104-105 1 Tom Leighton, 2-12 James Mortimer; 106-109 James Mortimer; 110 John Vaughan; 114-115 Marco de Valdivia; 116-117 James Wedge; 118-119 John Vaughan; 120 Max Forsythe; 121 Fritz von der Schulenburg; 122-124 Kevin Summers; 125 Richard Bryant; 126 James Mortimer; 127 Richard Bryant; 128-129 Jacques Dirand; 130 above Dan Cornish; 130 below Deidi von Schaewen; 131 James Mortimer; 132-134 Deidi von Schaewen; 135 John Vaughan; 136 Richard Davies; 140 James Mortimer; 141-142 Lucinda Lambton; 143-145 James Mortimer; 146 C. S. Sykes; 147 above left C. S. Sykes; 147 above right Richard Davies; 147 centre left Fritz von der Schulenburg; 148 Richard Davies; 149 C. S. Sykes; 150-151 Fritz von der Schulenburg; 152 Isidoro Genovese; 153 Lucinda Lambton; 154 C. S. Sykes; 154-155 Fritz von der Schulenburg; 156-157 James Mortimer; 158 Lucinda Lambton; 159 John Vere Brown; 160 above left James Mortimer; 160 centre left François Halard; 160 below left and below centre Tim Beddow; 160-162 John Vere Brown; 163 Fritz von der Schulenburg; 164-167 James Mortimer; 168-171 Fritz von der Schulenburg; 172 François Halard; 173 above left Fritz von der Schulenburg; 173 above right C. S. Sykes; 173 centre left François Halard; 173 centre right James Mortimer; 174 above left Fritz von der Schulenburg; 174 above right John Vere Brown; 174 below left C. S. Sykes; 174 below right Fritz von der Schulenburg; 175 Isidoro Genovese; 176-177 Richard Davies; 178 Ingalill Snitt; 182-5 James Mortimer; 186 David Gamble; 187 Tom Leighton; 188-189 John Vere Brown; 190-193 François Halard; 194-195 James Mortimer; 196 Fritz von der Schulenburg; 197 Richard Davies; 198-201 James Mortimer; 202-203 Peo Eriksson; 204-205 1 Peo Eriksson, 2-5 Ingalill Snitt, 6 Peo Eriksson, 7 Ingalill Snitt, 8 Peo Eriksson, 9-11 Ingalill Snitt; 206-207 Jean Pierre Godeaut; 208-209 John Vaughan; 209 above David Gamble; 209 below James Mortimer; 210-211 David Gamble; 212-213 James Mortimer; 213 right François Halard; 214-215 James Mortimer; 216 James Wedge; 220-221 Tim Beddow; 222 Kevin Summers; 223 James Mortimer; 224 James Wedge; 225 François Halard; 226 Tim Beddow; 227 James Wedge; 228-229 Lucinda Lambton; 230 Tim Beddow; 231 James Wedge; 232-234 James Mortimer; 235 above C. S. Sykes; 235 below James Mortimer; 236 James Mortimer; 240-241 John Vere Brown; 242-243 James Mortimer; 243 Richard Davies; 244 James Mortimer; 245 left, above and below Fritz von der Schulenburg; 245 right, above and below James Mortimer; 246-249 James Mortimer; 250-251 Lucinda Lambton; 252-253 James Mortimer.